Get a Grip on Network Cabling

Get a Grip on Network Cabling

Frank J. Derfler, Jr., and Les Freed

Ziff-Davis Press
Emeryville, California

Editor	Kate Hoffman
Technical Reviewer	Mark Johnston
Project Coordinator	Sheila McGill
Editorial Assistant	Cori Pansarasa
Proofreader	Cort Day
Cover Photograph	Roberto Brosan
Cover Design	Carrie English
Book Design	Paper Crane Graphics, Berkeley
Technical Illustration	Cherie Plumlee Computer Graphics & Illustration
Word Processing	Howard Blechman, Cat Haglund, and Allison Levin
Page Layout	Tony Jonick and Anna L. Marks
Indexer	Valerie Robbins

Ziff-Davis Press books are produced on a Macintosh computer system with the following applications: FrameMaker®, Microsoft® Word, QuarkXPress®, Adobe Illustrator®, Adobe Photoshop®, Adobe Streamline™, MacLink®Plus, Aldus® FreeHand™, Collage Plus™.

Ziff-Davis Press
5903 Christie Avenue
Emeryville, CA 94608

ISBN 1-56276-057-2

Manufactured in the United States of America
10 9 8 7 6 5 4

This book is dedicated to those who still like to get their hands on the hardware! We both learned to strip wire at about the same time we learned to ride bicycles and our fascination with bent metal continues. For those who can appreciate cabling as an art form: Enjoy!

K9KIC and WA4DFO

■ Contents at a Glance

■ Table of Contents

xiii

■ Acknowledgments

Willy and the folks at OK Cable follow in the steps of "Gus" at the Model Garage and Herb S. Brier's "Carl and Jerry" stories from decades ago. In more modern times, we wish to thank Steve Rigney and the Destin Lab Group for inspiration and perspiration. Mark Johnston provided valuable insight on standards and more practical issues. The folks at Amp, Anixter, and Mod-Tap responded in every possible way and we thank them for their help. At ZD Press, Kate Hoffman and Sheila McGill helped to bring the words and ideas into form and get them into your hands.

■ Introduction

Compared to other investments you'll make in computer products, your LAN cabling lasts practically forever! Software seems to go through an evolution every 2 to 3 years, and according to accountants, PC hardware is supposed to last for 5 years, but you will live for 15 years or more with your network cabling. The investment you make in a cabling scheme today will pay back dividends for years, but the rate of return you earn on your investment will depend on how wisely you choose the pieces and parts and supervise the installation of your cabling.

Our goal in writing this book is to prepare you either to make your own informed choices about cabling or to help you evaluate plans proposed by others. This is a practical book for people faced with tough, long-term decisions. It is as technical as it needs to be, but stresses practical tips and objective product information. We want this book to have as long and useful a life as your cabling system!

■ A Fundamental Investment

Cabling is "plugged in" at the most fundamental level of networking. The powerful computer hardware, the complex networking software, and the modules that implement sophisticated error-control and network-management protocols will sit idle because one whisker-thin piece of wire touches another in a space behind a wall, or because a little-used ventilation motor starts up and generates an electrical field that creates noise in the LAN cable. Your network can never be more reliable or perform better than its cabling allows.

There is a lot of similarity between investing money in your retirement fund and making an investment in LAN cabling. Putting your money in a mutual fund is the equivalent of adopting a wiring scheme built on standard principles developed by a major corporation such as IBM or AT&T. You can use the services of a consultant to guide your investment choices for both your retirement account and your cabling service; or, if you are well-informed, you can pick and choose from among complex options to make your own customized plan.

■ A Quick Look at the Contents

In Chapter 1 we'll give you an overview of networking technology and describe some of the economic and technical forces that shape your cabling options. Chapter 2 describes and categorizes the different types of cabling you can buy. Because cabling is part of a building structure as well as a part of the network, it is subject to an extraordinary number of descriptions, specifications, regulations, and standards. We describe those standards and buzz words in Chapter 3. Chapter 4 links cabling into the specifications of real networking systems like Ethernet and Token-Ring. In Chapter 5 we describe the important and quickly evolving wiring hubs that bring network management, statistical reporting, and improved reliability to your LAN cabling system.

Chapters 6, 7, 8, and 9 deal with products, tips, and techniques, and get into the detailed "hands-on" and "how to" descriptions of bringing wire into a central facility and applying the wide range of connectors. Chapter 7 specifically covers the important topic of power and grounding, and Chapter 9 describes options for fiber-optic cabling.

After you install the cabling, you must make sure it will work properly and reliably. Chapter 10 deals with cable testing and installation certification.

Chapter 11 doesn't deal with cabling at all! Instead, this chapter describes your options for wireless communications systems that might or might not include segments of copper or fiber-optic cabling.

- *Cable and Wire*
- *Above the Cable*
- *Protocols and Procedures*
- *Evolutionary Changes*
- *The Costs of Cabling*
- *Looking Upstream*

1

The Role of Cabling: Planning Considerations

The first thing Willy Barnett noticed was the silence. He had been here only once before, but people who had then been busy answering the phones and booking reservations were now turning the pages of magazines or talking together quietly in the corners of the room. Even before he found the network administrator, Willy saw the error message on the bottom of a computer screen: "Server Not Found."

The network administrator looked like a man with a migraine. "We're losing money by the minute, Willy. We've got all the phones on busy because it doesn't do any good to tell people we can't do business while the network is down. We've checked the hardware and software on the servers and they seem okay. Our network management programs rely on the network being up, so they don't work. I think the problem must be in the network cabling, but it's nothing I can find."

OK Cable, Willy's company, hadn't installed this network cabling. The original installers weren't even in the phone book anymore. Having no diagrams of the cable layout, he decided to start at the closest point and pulled a PC away from the wall. Then he took a small meter about the size of a deck of playing cards out of his pocket, applied the leads to the Ethernet connector, and grunted.

"Fifty ohms. You've got a cable break. Anybody move their desks around last night or this morning?" The wordless network administrator shook his head and shifted his feet as though he were walking on hot coals.

Willy searched the offices for the last PC on the thin Ethernet cable, the one with a terminating resistor. When he found it, he attached a device about the size of a paperback novel to the cable. Within a few seconds the liquid crystal screen flashed: "Cable open at 90 feet."

Moving about 40 feet across the office, Willy reached in back of a PC. When he touched a connector with smooth flat sides, he rolled his eyes and said: "I'll bet on this one. A twist-on connector. A problem waiting to happen."

As he talked, he clipped off the old connector with a careful right-angle cut and used a special wire-stripping tool to take off just the right amounts of cable jacket, shielding braid, and inner insulation. Then he used a formidable-looking black crimping tool to create a permanent physical bond between the cable and a new connector. He attached the cable to its T-connector, used the little ohm meter again, and announced, "Twenty-five ohms. You're back on the air."

Following OK Cable policy, Willy presented an invoice before leaving the job. When he looked at the bill, the network administrator said: "I don't pay my lawyer this much an hour!" The old punch line, "That's why I gave up law," passed through Willy's mind, but he decided to take a different approach.

"You're either going to pay me now or pay me later," he said. "You've bet your business on a network cabling system that can fail from any one of three or four causes including twist-on connectors, people who don't know how to

disconnect a PC from the cable without taking the whole network down, and a cable installation that exceeds the maximum recommended length by 100 feet. This won't be the last bill you'll get for an emergency call if you don't make some changes." The network administrator sighed, closed his office door, and said to Willy: "Let's talk."

■ Introduction

LANs spread. In the late 1980s, the typical local area network had fewer than five nodes, all within a small office area of well under 1,000 square feet. In the 1990s, the majority (58% in 1993) of PCs used in business and government are connected to networks, and the networks have infiltrated every distant corner of the building or campus. Many modern local networks cover areas measured in square miles.

Small networks typically have simple cabling requirements. A piece of wire thrown along the baseboard behind the desks often does the job. But, as networks grow in size, the cabling system takes bigger parts of the budget, planning activities, and administrators' time. Also, because networks can use different LAN adapters, networking software, and applications over the same cable, the cabling system becomes the common denominator and thus the base of sophisticated network-management technologies.

Often the first and most definitive decision to make about a network is the type of wiring to use. Starting out on the wrong course can incur future penalties in time, money, or performance, as the network grows. Follow along and we'll describe the ways cabling systems fit into the architecture of a network and the relative costs and long-term importance of cabling systems.

■ Cable and Wire

Throughout this book, when we use the term *network cabling,* usually we mean copper wire twisted or shielded inside an outer jacket made of plastic. In many cases, however, the jacket will surround strands of plastic or glass that conduct light in much the same way that copper conducts electricity. When we refer to *cable,* we use the term's most generic meaning: the stuff that conducts signals between network nodes. We'll be specific when referring to the various types of cable, such as shielded or unshielded twisted-pair wire, coaxial cable, or fiber-optic cable. The word *wire* typically refers to individual copper wires with a cable jacket.

■ Above the Cable

It's easier to understand networks if you think of each element above the cabling as a process. Each element takes data in at one end, processes it, and then passes it out at the other end. The purpose of the processing is to package or unpackage the data going to and from the network connections.

In any model of network operations, such as the one shown in Figure 1.1, every other block in the diagram depends on and is supported by the network cabling. The cabling—sometimes referred to in academic circles as *transmission medium* or *network media*—is separate from, but tightly linked to, the rest of the operational components of the network. If you want to understand the details and alternatives of the network elements above the cable, we recommend the *PC Magazine Guide to Connectivity, Second Edition,* Ziff-Davis Press, 1992.

LAN Adapters

The cabling itself connects to LAN adapters in the various network nodes. Some LAN adapters are separate printed-circuit boards designed for computers that range in size from desktop PCs, to IBM AS/400 midframe machines, to the communications controllers for IBM mainframe computers. Well over two hundred companies market LAN adapters for PCs, and their products have street prices that range from $100 to $700. An illustrated example of a LAN adapter is shown in Figure 1.2.

Some companies make LAN adapters a part of the PC. For example, Zenith Data Systems builds a LAN adapter into every laptop and desktop PC in their product line. If the PC doesn't have a built-in adapter or an expansion slot to add a circuit board, then you can use an external LAN adapter like those marketed by D-Link Systems or Xircom Corporation.

Because the LAN adapter must have some specific circuitry to connect to the type of cable used in the network, the selection of the cabling can drive the selection of the LAN adapter. Many adapters, however, like Zenith's built-ins, have circuitry for several types of cabling.

HINT. *You must choose LAN adapters that are compatible with the type of cable, the type of computer expansion bus, and the type of networking software you use. Make a careful inventory of your computers and settle on your cabling scheme before you buy your LAN adapters. Chapter 2 discusses the various types of cabling.*

Each LAN adapter has three important jobs to do in its interconnection to the network cable:

• Making a physical connection

Figure 1.1

This block diagram shows the functional elements of a client PC and file server. Note that the powerful processors and software, designed according to elegant protocols, are all linked by a thin piece of cable.

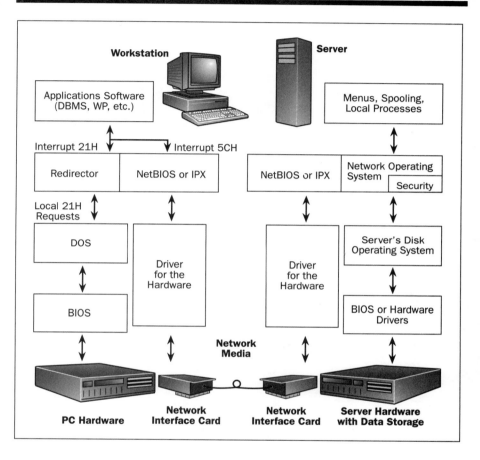

- Providing electrical signaling

- Implementing orderly access to the shared network cable system

The Physical Connection

The physical connection depends on one of several types of cable connectors. (We'll describe the types and give instructions on how to install the most commonly used connectors in Chapter 7.) The most common types are shown in Figure 1.3. Generally, these connectors use a male plug on the cable and a female jack on the chassis of the computer or LAN adapter. They physically lock with a snap or a twist for a solid connection.

Figure 1.2

This typical Ethernet LAN adapter inserts into an industry-standard architecture (IBM PC AT architecture) expansion bus. It connects to thin Ethernet cabling through its BNC connector or to an external transceiver (for other types of cables) through its attachment-unit interface (AUI) port.

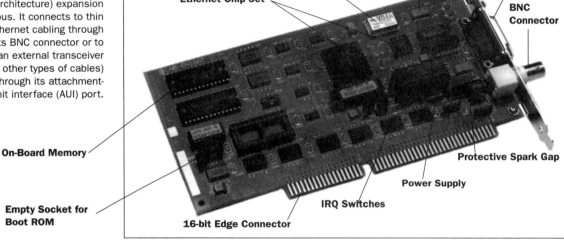

AUI/BNC Jumpers

AUI Connector

Timing Crystal

BNC Connector

Ethernet Chip Set

On-Board Memory

Protective Spark Gap

Power Supply

Empty Socket for Boot ROM

IRQ Switches

16-bit Edge Connector

Figure 1.3

The most widely used types of network cable connectors are (from left to right): a BNC connector on coaxial cable, an ST fiber-optic connector on fiber-optic cables, an IBM type 1 connector on shielded twisted-pair wiring, and an RJ-45 connector on unshielded twisted-pair wire.

NOTE. *Connectors are the weakest links in a network cable system. Poorly installed connectors can create electrical noise, make intermittent electrical contact, and disrupt the network. It pays to invest in the best connectors and installation tools.*

Baseband and Broadband Signaling

Copper network cables carry electrical signals, while fiber-optic cables carry pulses of light. In the 1980s, two technologies competed for popularity in the copper cable market: baseband and broadband signaling.

In broadband signaling—the more technically elegant signaling technique—each LAN adapter treats the network cable like a radio antenna. Each broadband LAN adapter is a small radio-transmitting and -receiving station that pumps a broad spectrum of radio-frequency energy into the cable. This scheme uses complex radio repeaters and requires careful installation and frequent maintenance. These disadvantages far outweigh the advertised advantage of broadband signaling: the ability to combine voice, video, and data on the same network cable. New installations of broadband systems are very rare, and we won't discuss them further in this book.

Baseband signaling uses a direct-current voltage, very similar to the voltage of a car battery, to signal the presence of a digital 0 or a 1 on the cable. The adapter applies a positive or a negative voltage in the range of +15 to −15 volts to the cable, and the transition between the voltage levels indicates a change from one binary state to the other.

The peak of each positive and negative cycle is flat, generating the picture of square waves. But, as these square waves travel over the cable, the electrical capacitance and inductance in the cable drag at the voltage and the current of the signal and round off its square edges. The factors create *attenuation*—reduction in the amplitude of the positive and negative voltages.

Faster signaling speeds put even more stringent demands on cabling systems. The higher speeds decrease the time duration between the square waves and make it more difficult for the LAN adapters to discriminate between them.

Higher-quality copper cables and connectors have more favorable capacitance, inductance, and resistance ratings and do less to round off and attenuate square waves. In later chapters, we'll describe the qualitative differences between copper cables and connectors with different ratings.

Sharing the Cable

"Networks are for sharing" is a phrase that you'll find in all our books. Local area networks allow people to share data and program files, devices such as printers and CD-ROM drives, and communications links to other computers and LANs. But sharing starts with the network cabling scheme. On a shared cable, only one node can transmit at a time, so each LAN adapter gives its network node orderly access to the network cable by following a specific *media-access control (MAC)* scheme. MAC is an operational scheme recognized by modern standards committees.

The three most common MAC schemes are described in the ARCnet, Ethernet, and Token-Ring standards. We'll describe the specific cabling schemes associated with each standard in Chapter 4. You don't have to consider the operation of the MAC layer to select a cabling scheme, but understanding the MAC layer will help you to understand why some wiring systems are laid out in specific ways.

■ Protocols and Procedures

Protocols are agreements among different parts of the network on how data are to be transferred. They describe how things work. Committees established by organizations such as the Institute of Electrical and Electronics Engineers (IEEE), the Electronic Industries Association (EIA), and International Consultive Committee on Telephone and Telegraph (CCITT in French) typically labor for years to develop these agreements on how electronic devices signal, exchange data, and handle problems. Committees develop protocols, but companies develop products conforming to those protocols. Some companies, particularly IBM, used to establish their own proprietary protocols and products (at least partially in an attempt to lock customers into their technology), but today, so-called open systems of protocols, established by national and international committees, prevail.

In theory, if a company develops a product that operates according to a standard protocol, the product will work with products from all other vendors meeting that same standard. In practice, companies often implement the protocols in ways so different that the products don't work together without a lot of adjustment on both sides. However, the concept of compatibility among LAN products is sound, and constant improvement efforts are working.

There are three standard protocols for network cabling and media access control that should interest you: Ethernet, Token-Ring, and ARCnet. A few companies, usually in the low-cost LAN market, still sell adapters following protocols that aren't approved or that do not even adhere to de facto standards. Generally, we urge you not to buy LAN adapters that don't use one of the standard protocol sets. The small up-front savings you might enjoy open you to the risk of owning an orphan system without support and without the ability to expand.

Ethernet

The primary characteristics of the physical Ethernet link include

- A data rate of 10 megabits per second

- A maximum station separation of 2.8 kilometers

- A shielded coaxial cable connecting the stations

- A specific kind of electrical signaling on the cable called Manchester-encoded digital baseband.

The latter specification describes the electrical signals that make up the digital 0s and 1s that are constantly passing over the network. Ethernet uses a *broadcast architecture;* every node receives every broadcast from every other node at the same time.

Though Ethernet's data-transmission speed is rated at 10 megabits per second, research by Digital Equipment Corporation and other companies shows that even heavily used networks with multiple servers do not average more than a few megabits per second under normal loads. That load factor will increase as more applications, particularly specialized workgroup productivity systems and applications using large files of bitmapped graphics, use the network.

The CSMA-CD Media Access Control Protocol

The major part of the data-link layer specification for Ethernet describes the way stations share access to coaxial cable through a process called Carrier Sense Multiple Access with Collision Detection (CSMA/CD). CSMA/CD is a media access control (MAC) protocol that determines how nodes on the network share access to the cable. The medium is the coaxial cable connecting the network nodes, and the access control protocol is the sharing scheme. Before packets of information can traverse the cable of the Ethernet network, they must deal with CSMA/CD.

CSMA/CD works in a listen-before-transmit mode: If the network adapter receives data to send from higher-level software, it checks to see if any other station is broadcasting on the cable. Only when the cable is clear does the network adapter broadcast its message.

CSMA/CD also mediates when the inevitable happens: Two or more nodes simultaneously start to transmit on an idle cable and the transmissions collide. The adapters can detect such collisions because of the higher electrical-signal level that simultaneous transmissions produce. When they detect a collision, the network adapter cards begin transmitting what is called a jam signal to ensure that all the conflicting nodes notice the collision. Then, each adapter stops transmitting and goes to its internal programming to determine a randomly selected time for retransmission. This "back-off" period ensures that the stations don't continue to send out colliding signals every time the cable grows quiet.

The 802.3 10BaseT Standard

In late 1990, after three years of meetings, proposals, and compromises, a committee of the IEEE finalized a specification for running Ethernet-type signaling over twisted-pair wiring.

The IEEE calls the standard "802.3i 10BaseT". The IEEE 802.3-standards family generally describes CSMA signaling, like Ethernet, used over various wiring systems. The 10BaseT name indicates a signaling speed of 10 megabits per second, a baseband signaling scheme, and twisted-pair wiring in a star physical topology.

The theoretical and widely touted appeal of the 10BaseT standard is that it gives LAN managers the option to use installed telephone wiring, thereby saving installation problems and costs. Keeping things simple and inexpensive is a nice objective, but, unfortunately, the roadblocks you find in most real installations cause complications.

Many organizations don't have existing wiring with the right electrical characteristics to support a network installation, so LAN planners often find they must pull more wire anyway. The technology of unshielded twisted-pair wiring, however, unlike coaxial Ethernet alternatives and Token-Ring's shielded twisted-pair, is familiar to technicians you already have on staff or on contract. As we found during testing in the PC Magazine LAN Labs, the strong practical appeal of 10BaseT products is in their commonality. You can safely mix and match 10BaseT adapter cards and wiring hubs from many companies and use them together on the same network. This commonality provides you with multiple sources of supply, confidence in long-term support, and competitive prices. Our PC Magazine LAN Labs testing also proved that you don't pay a performance penalty for using 10BaseT twisted-pair. Our throughput tests showed consistent performance, as good as you get with coaxial-cable Ethernet wiring.

The biggest potential advantage of a 10BaseT wiring installation to a network manager comes from the star-cabling scheme. The star-wiring scheme (the general configuration is shown in Figure 1.4) provides both reliability and centralized management. Like spokes from the hub of a wheel, the wires go from a central wiring-hub out to each node. If one wire run is broken or shorted, that node is out of commission, but the network remains operational. In station-to-station wiring schemes like thin Ethernet, one bad connection at any point takes down the entire network.

Figure 1.4

The IEEE 10BaseT architecture uses a central wiring hub and a separate run of cable to each node. In this diagram, the wiring is terminated on a punchdown block to improve its accessibility. One PC uses a media access unit (MAU) or external transceiver to make the connection to unshielded twisted-pair wire.

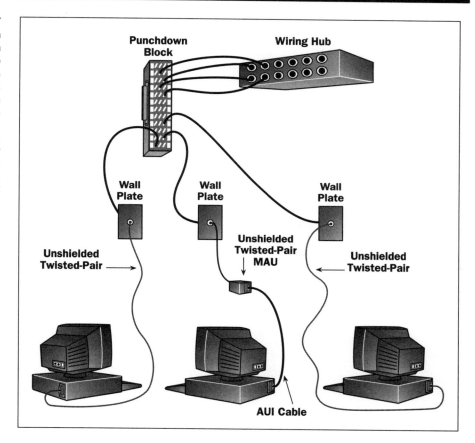

Size Considerations

Because of the carrier-sense media-access control system, every Ethernet adapter must "hear" at least part of every packet transmitted by any other adapter on the same network at the same time. Imagine three nodes, one each at either end and one at the center of a very, very long cable. Suppose the adapter at one end of the cable sends a short packet of data that goes completely by the center node before its front end reaches the distant node. When the packet clears the center node, the adapter at the center sees a quiet cable and immediately sends out its own packet. Together, the near and center nodes can foreclose any opportunity for the end node to transmit. If an adapter is so far away from the point of origin that, even at nearly the speed of light, the front part of the packet doesn't reach it before the back of the packet clears all other nodes, the chance exists for conflict. So, in

Ethernet, the maximum cable distance is a factor of the minimum packet size and the usable strength of the signal.

Overall, the rules for a thin Ethernet cable segment say that the system can have 185 meters (606 feet) of cable before it must have a repeater. Only 30 nodes can populate a single thin-cable segment, and there must be a minimum of .5 meters (2 feet) of cable between each node.

The star wiring configuration of the 10BaseT wiring scheme changes the rules. Each cable segment linking the 10BaseT wiring hub and a network node can have a maximum length of 100 meters (328 feet), although some hub manufacturers advertise that their equipment can work over greater distances. The 10BaseT system offers approximately the same end-to-end distance as thin Ethernet; but because of the hub-and-spoke design, its coverage in a radius around the wiring hub is much greater.

ARCnet

The ARCnet system, originated by Datapoint Corporation and fostered in the microcomputer world by Standard Microsystems Corporation, uses messages addressed to specific stations to regulate traffic. The ARC acronym stands for Datapoint's Attached Resource Computing architecture. You can buy ARCnet adapters through the mail-order pages of *PC Magazine* for under $75, yet the throughput and reliability of these adapters are generally excellent. Like Ethernet, ARCnet uses a broadcast architecture in which all stations receive all messages broadcast into the cable at approximately the same time, without action by any other node. This is in contrast to the repeater activity of nodes in the Token-Ring system.

Recent Developments

Two interesting things happened on the ARCnet front. First, in October 1992, the American National Standards Institute (ANSI) specified the ARCnet protocol as the "ATA/ANSI 878.1 Local Area Network Standard." There is no IEEE committee working on ARCnet because the formal role of the IEEE is to design a standard, whereas ANSI standardizes an existing specification, and the ARCnet specification dates from the 1960s. As a similar example, fiber distributed data interface (FDDI) is not an IEEE standard but it is an ANSI standard, and FDDI is widely accepted. Organizations that follow the policy of buying products that follow open standards can now refer to that ANSI ARCnet standard in their requests for bids.

The second interesting happening in the ARCnet world is Datapoint's introduction of ARCNETPLUS, which provides signaling at 20 megabits per second that can be intermixed with existing 2.5 megabit-per-second ARCnet wiring systems, hubs, and adapters. You can put ARCNETPLUS in the nodes that can benefit from faster service while leaving the rest of the network unchanged.

For example, for $695 you can replace the old-style ARCnet adapter you presently have in a file server with a Datapoint ARCNETPLUS LAN adapter, and it will service intermixed requests from both 2.5 megabit and 20 megabit adapters. You can equip the few fast PCs that need high-speed network access with 20 megabit adapters and never touch the rest of the nodes. You must upgrade any ARCnet wiring hub that is the first point of contact for a 20 megabit adapter, but you don't have to upgrade intervening hubs. For $1195, Datapoint sells a hub card that fits into a PC and provides four ports and also serves as the host PC's ARCNETPLUS LAN connection.

We still like ARCnet. ARCnet works reliably, and the 2.5 megabit-per-second signaling speed is not a limitation in typical office installations. Few PCs can move data faster than 1.2 megabits per second under the most ideal and demanding conditions. The adoption of the ANSI standard plus the introduction of 20 megabit service that intermixes with existing nodes add to the modern appeal of this proven technology.

The technical literature describes ARCnet as a token-passing system, but it operates very differently from IEEE 802.5 Token-Ring. Instead of passing a token from station to station, one station broadcasts the transmission permission message to the others on the network.

Each Ethernet and Token-Ring adapter has a unique adapter identifier assigned by the manufacturer and drawn from a common pool established by industry associations. ARCnet adapters, however, don't come with an identification number assigned. You set the identification number, from 1 to 255, using switches located on each adapter. The identification numbers have no relationship to the position of the nodes on the cable or to any other physical positioning factor.

When activated, the adapters broadcast their numbers, and the lowest-numbered active station becomes the controller for the network. This controller sends a token to each active station, granting permission to transmit. When each station receives the permission token, it either sends its waiting message or remains silent. After a pause of a few milliseconds, the controlling station sends a permission token to the next station in numeric sequence.

HINT. *Keep your assigned ARCnet station numbers close together and put PCs with the most powerful CPUs in the low-numbered slots. The polling task takes a tiny bit of CPU power, so put your husky servers and other fast PCs into position to take on that role.*

When a new station enters the network, the stations all rebroadcast their station numbers in what is called a reconfiguration or "recon." Like the collisions in Ethernet, the concept of a recon bothers people who worry about esoteric matters of network efficiency. In reality, a recon takes no longer than, in the worst case, 65 milliseconds and scarcely disturbs the flow of traffic on a network.

NOTE. *There are two things an ARCnet installer can't afford to lose: the instruction manual telling how to set the adapter numbers and the list of adapter numbers active on the network. If you know what station numbers are assigned, it's easy to add more stations. If you don't know what station numbers are active, you face a frustrating session of research or trial-and-error installation.*

The Topology

The ARCnet scheme traditionally uses RG/62 coaxial cable in a star physical topology—the star topology allows for a hierarchy of hubs. Small two- or four-port wiring hubs can feed other large and small hubs in an economical wiring scheme that retains the resistance to total outage inherent in a star topology.

The RG/62 cable specified for ARCnet is the same cable used by IBM in its 3270 wiring plan that links terminals to mainframe computers. Since this plan also uses a star topology, many companies find it easy to install ARCnet when they downsize their computer systems from IBM mainframes to networks of PCs. They can keep the same coaxial-cable wiring in place and replace the IBM mainframe communications controller with a simple wiring hub. Modern versions of ARCnet can also use coaxial cable or unshielded twisted-pair wire in a station-to-station physical topology.

High-impedance ARCnet adapters allow a station-to-station physical topology identical to thin Ethernet. However, the station-to-station nodes can also connect to active powered hubs for an overall network of 20,000 feet of cable—approximately twenty times the distance of thin Ethernet.

Size Considerations

A complex set of rules regulates how big an ARCnet network can be. Generally, the maximum length of cable from one end of the network to the other is 20,000 feet. The maximum cable length to regenerate signals between *powered,* or so-called *active* hubs, is 2,000 feet. The length between a powered hub and a network node is also 2,000 feet. Unpowered passive hubs can connect to nodes over 100 feet of cable. As you can see, ARCnet systems can cover a large geographical area.

NOTE. *A general rule of communications is that you trade speed for distance. Architectures, like ACRnet, that use slower signaling can span greater cable lengths without the need for a repeater. Faster 10 megabit-per-second Ethernet and 16 megabit-per-second Token-Ring carry increasingly stringent cable-length limitations.*

Several companies, including PureData and Standard Microcomputer Systems, offer fiber-optic versions of ARCnet systems. These systems have the typical fiber-optic characteristics of low electrical emissions, low absorption of electrical noise, and extended distance.

Token-Ring

The Token-Ring concept and its underlying cabling plan evolved at IBM in the period from 1982 to 1985. Since then, Token-Ring has become the central supporting pillar of IBM connectivity. The company markets Token-Ring adapters and software for every level of computer product. The Token-Ring system is described in an open IEEE standard 802.5, but the standardization process was guided and led by people from IBM.

If you're going to "bet the business" on your network, you want it to be reliable and robust. Token-Ring uses a precise mechanism called token-passing for regulating the access of each node to the cable. The nodes on the network pass a small message called a token from station to station on a ring of cable. When a node has data to transmit, it changes the free token to a busy token and sends the data from its application program inside a formatted package called a "frame." Each node on the ring repeats each bit of the frame as it is received, but only the addressee copies the frame to a buffer on the LAN adapter and then into the host device. When the originating node receives its busy token from upstream in the ring, it turns it back into a free token and sends it into the ring downstream.

The real system is, of course, much more complex. Here's what is actually involved:

- The adapter cards learn the addresses of their upstream neighbors to speed recovery from interruptions.

- The station with the highest internal address (assigned during manufacture of the adapter) acts as a monitor to keep the token going, and a secondary station monitors the activity of the primary monitor.

- Built-in problem determination procedures (PDPs) identify a malfunctioning adapter and remove it from the ring.

The token-passing technique stands in stark contrast to the comparative free-for-all of the somewhat older Ethernet CSMA/CD standard, in which a node listens for a break in the traffic and tries to insert data onto the network cable before any other node.

Token-Ring is designed to survive. While this system is electrically a ring, it is physically a star with cabling reaching out to each node from a central wiring hub. This configuration is shown in Figure 1.5. The wiring hub uses a relay to sense voltage coming from an adapter after the adapter has passed a rigorous self-test and is ready to enter the ring. The hub actually breaks the electrical continuity of the ring for a fraction of a second while it switches in the new entrant. In Token-Ring terminology, a wiring center is a multistation access unit (MAU) or, in an improved version, a controlled access unit (CAU). Dozens of companies market MAUs and CAUs with different capabilities, including elaborate management and reporting schemes and the ability to extend communications over longer-than-recommended cable spans.

Figure 1.5

The Token-Ring architecture uses a star-wiring configuration, although the data passes from node to node around an electrical ring. This diagram shows various wiring centers, including two-port hubs that allow you to share a single cable run to the wiring center between two nodes in the same office.

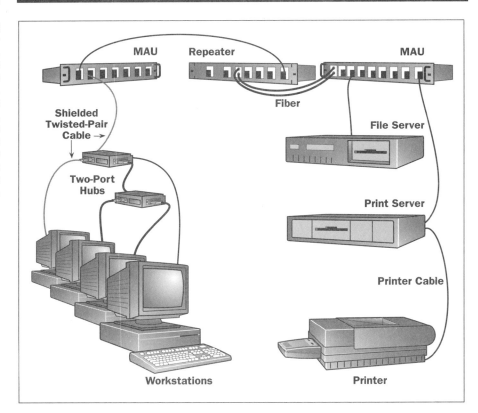

The Wiring Hub

Because of the wiring hub, damage to a cable run going to an inactive station never affects the nodes in the active ring. If an adapter fails, or something happens to the cable going to an adapter, that piece of the ring is immediately discarded.

The system becomes more complex as you link wiring hubs together. The hubs maintain the ring architecture for the flow of data in one extended network, even though the wiring hubs are in different work areas or wiring closets several hundred feet apart. In practice, one ring can have many wiring centers, and the wiring centers are often spread around the building. When two separate wiring centers are linked, a physical diagram of them would look like two stars reaching out toward each other.

The Token-Ring standard allows for either 4 or 16 megabit-per-second signaling speeds, and new LAN adapters that you'll buy will typically be able to operate at either speed. However, you can't intermix the 4 and 16 megabit signals on the same network. In practice, many companies use 16 megabit-per-second signaling between wiring hubs and 4 megabit-per-second signaling from the wiring hub to the network nodes.

Chapter 5 is dedicated to the topic of hubs and repeaters.

Cabling Alternatives

As we'll describe in Chapter 4, the IEEE 802.5 Token-Ring standards give you a lot of leeway to choose cabling alternatives. The original specification called for a cable made from shielded twisted-pair wire (STP). STP provides a high-quality electrical environment, and it can easily handle the 4 or 16 megabit-per-second signaling of Token-Ring and also be suitable for emerging 100 megabit-per-second systems. But this cable is bulky and quickly fills wiring conduits.

While IBM tried to stick to shielded twisted-pair, users in general clamored for the unshielded twisted-pair (UTP) used in high-end telephone systems and in the IEEE 802.3 10BaseT. The primary appeal of UTP is its small size; it doesn't clog wiring ducts. IBM initially specified an unshielded twisted-pair cable as IBM Type 3 cable. Type 3 cable works reliably in 4 megabit-per-second service, but it must be carefully installed to work reliably in 16 megabit-per-second systems. In Chapter 3, we describe newer UTP standards for high-speed Token-Ring installations.

UTP was certainly never in IBM's original plans for reliable connectivity wiring, but the company has joined with Synoptics Communications to get IEEE approval for a plan using passive inductive and capacitive circuits to properly form the signal for transmission over UTP at 16 megabits per second. They have also released a family of Lobe Attachment Modules that can link shielded and unshielded twisted-pair cable. (Each run of cable from a hub to a node is called a *lobe.*)

Size Considerations

Complicated formulas guide the number of wiring centers, the cable distance between them, the number of nodes, and the maximum length of cable between a wiring center and a node. In the simplest form, any single ring is limited to a maximum of 72 nodes on UTP and a maximum of 260 nodes on

So, if you have more nodes—or if you simply want to limit the traffic on any one ring—you link the rings with a Token-Ring bridge. The bridge passes traffic between rings, re-inserting only certain frames into the downstream ring to reduce the amount of traffic and to avoid ring-size and cable-length limitations.

■ Evolutionary Changes

Until the early 1990s, choosing a specific networking standard like ARCnet or Token-Ring automatically dictated the type of copper cable and the physical configuration of the cabling system you could use for your network. But buyers and sellers want to have their cake and eat it at the same time; they want standardized systems but also flexibility. So vendors began offering LAN adapters with options for cabling schemes that did and did not meet the standard; and then, in many cases, vendors set out to expand the standard as well.

In the mid-1990s, we have standards with many options for cabling. This flexibility doesn't reduce the need for careful planning and good installation, but it does mean that you can use different types of cable, like twisted-pair wire, coaxial cable, and fiber-optic cable, with any type popular network-access protocols and signaling.

■ The Costs of Cabling

Let's examine the costs of installing a 20-node local area network to illustrate how the cost of cabling can be a wildcard factor in your budget. The major cost elements you'll have in this installation are the server, the networking software, the LAN adapters, and the cabling.

While the prices of PCs suitable for use as servers continue to drop, we haven't seen such a dramatic slide in the price of hard-disk-drive storage. So, for $5,000 you can expect to buy a computer with a fast processor, at least 16 megabytes of RAM for disk caching, and over 300 megabytes of disk storage. The networking software will average around $250 per client, or another $5,000 for a 20-node network. It is reasonable to price the LAN adapter cards at $150 each, even if they are built into the PC, so figure about $3,200 for the network, including a few dollars for a more capable adapter in the server. Note that Token-Ring adapters might cost more than $300 each and that ARCnet adapters would probably cost under $100 each.

The cost of installing cabling is often the hidden surprise in networking. We'll start out with a wiring hub. The price for wiring hubs varies—Token-Ring is more and ARCnet is less—but the popular 10BaseT hubs usually cost a little less than $100 per port. You can pay much more for hubs with internal management systems, but we won't include that capability in this relatively small network. So, we will start the budget for cabling with $2,000 for wiring hubs.

Let's assume that this installation will use a fireproof cable with runs of 100 feet each. You will pay about $.20 per foot for this cable, so we will add $400 to the budget. Wall plates cost $4.75 each; a patch panel is $210; and there will probably be $50-worth of plastic wire wraps and connectors in the installation. So, we add another $350.

Labor is the biggest variable in the cost of cabling, and if you run into installation problems, it can be the biggest unpleasant surprise. Experience shows that it takes about 7 minutes to prepare each end of the cable, 20 minutes to run each cable, 1 hour to unpack and clean up, and 10 minutes per cable for certification. Add an hour for things that go wrong. If we assume $25 an hour for each of two people, you will pay at least $1,000 for labor. Thus, if everything goes smoothly, your bottom line will be close to $4,000— about $200 per node. Not included in this simple analysis are your other expenses, such as vehicles, licenses, training, tools, and test equipment. If it is difficult to run the wires through the walls of your building, or if your hourly labor rates are higher, the installation costs can skyrocket.

On the bottom line, you'll spend nearly $20,000 to network 20 computers, including the cost of an added server. The cabling is slightly less than 25% of that cost, but overall your network is no better than its cabling system. The cabling is critical to reliability and throughput, and a surprisingly large number of network problems are cabling problems. A good cabling installation costs more in the beginning, but pays dividends for years.

■ Looking Upstream

In the first half of the 1990s, networks have been lightly loaded; but that will change as the decade rolls on. New applications will drive the need for more throughput (more carrying capacity in the cabling system) and more flexibility.

The way people are using local area networks is changing. The networking model for the early 90s put all of the shared data and program files on a single server. The server might have been dedicated to that role or might also have been used as a personal workstation. In this model, the network traffic flows between the clients and the server, with the server generating most of the traffic. Typically, overall network traffic averaged no more than 10–15% of the total capacity of the network.

But, in the mid-1990s, a new networking model will emerge. As the number of networked PCs grows beyond 50%, you'll see a new model of distributed resource sharing. Practically all applications will be networked applications; most printers will be networked printers; and a great deal of workgroup-process information will be shared across the network. The work of the group will take place and be tracked on the network.

Techniques developed by Microsoft and IBM can link applications across the network. For example, let's assume that a workgroup is responsible for publishing a weekly report that includes text, spreadsheets, photos, drawings, and graphs. One person in the workgroup using a word processing program is responsible for preparing the text. Within the body of the text, the word processing program links to the output files from a second person's spreadsheet program, a third person's graphics program, and a fourth person's scanner into specific positions.

As the person creating the words moves through the text, the network-aware software brings in the latest versions of the files from wherever they are stored. The entire network becomes a large dynamic database for the preparation of the report. Similar linking-techniques can help workgroups as they take and fulfill orders, control manufacturing processes, schedule events, and share databases of thoughts. However, this type of processing generates a lot more network traffic than the old central-server model.

The first decade of networking and office automation, the 1980s, did little to reduce the amount of paper used in workgroups. In fact, it is often said that the principal output of a computer is paper. But, that will change in the second decade of networking. Computer displays will be better and more vivid than paper, and electronic networks will make digital images more portable than they are today. But all of these networked nodes will generate more network traffic.

The use of complex bitmapped graphics, the inclusion of digital images in electronic mail, and the integration of sound and images in multimedia presentations will also increase network traffic.

In short, there will be more data to move across the cables, so signaling rates will go up. This means for many network planners that they should not limit future growth by installing low-quality wire systems today.

But, along with faster signaling, people designing networks will demand more flexibility. For example, IBM, National Semiconductor, and Texas Instruments have single-chip sets that include the capabilities to use either the Ethernet or Token-Ring protocols over the network cable. These chip sets make it easier for manufacturers to put the LAN adapter on the PC's motherboard and offer either networking protocol, but they will also generate demands for more cabling and connector flexibility when the Ethernet/Token-Ring LAN-equipped PC arrives at a desktop.

The longer view shows even more of a mix of cabling and signaling on corporate local area networks. Digital Equipment Corporation and 3Com have announced new products for the 100 megabit-per-second fiber distributed data interface (FDDI) with lower prices, and the American National Standards Institute X3T9.5 committee is working on two architectures for 100 megabit transmission over unshielded twisted-pair wire. You don't need 100 megabit or even 16 megabit-per-second service to every node, but the future outlook shows the need for flexible and tailored connections in a tightly managed corporate environment.

- *Keeping Things In, Keeping Things Out*
- *Coaxial Cable*
- *Unshielded Twisted Pair (UTP)*
- *Shielded Twisted Pair (STP)*
- *Fiber-optic Cable*
- *Making Decisions*

2

Cable Basics

"Wire is wire, isn't that so?" the New Guy asked. "No," Willy replied patiently, "you can't run and you can't hide from the laws of physics. The laws of physics say there's a lot of difference between cables like these because of the size of the conductors, the kind of insulation between them, their arrangement inside the outer tubing, and their ability to keep out electrical noise."

Willy slid open another drawer and pulled out a rat's nest of cables the size of a wastebasket. (The New Guy was new at OK Cable partially because the guy before him hadn't kept his materials and installations neat.) Sloppy installations were bad installations in Willy's book. As he and the New Guy untangled the cables and marked them, Willy welcomed the opportunity to do some on-the-job training.

"The networks we put in are real finicky about their cabling. The faster the signaling speed of the LAN cards, the more finicky they get. Those're the laws of physics at work. As the signaling speed goes up, the square waves that represent the 0s and 1s on the wire are closer together, and it's more difficult for the LAN cards to tell them apart. If there is high electrical noise on the cable, or if a bad installation or bad design reduces the strength of the signals, the equipment can't detect the difference between a 0 and a 1, and the network is down."

"So everything depends on the cabling, huh?" the New Guy observed.

"Yup, time was when we really could run 1 megabit-per-second adapters like the old 10Net boards for a quarter mile over two strands of barbed wire. But today's 10, 16, and 100 megabit-per-second systems need high quality cable and careful installation."

Willy opened another drawer and pointed to more tangled cables. "Every connection counts, kid, every connection counts."

Wire, wire, everywhere and not an inch to link! All wire isn't cable and all cable isn't equal. Any single wire can be an individual conductor, but in electrical systems it takes two wires to form a complete circuit. When two or more wires are combined together in a manner that conforms to specific standards, we call the collective product a *cable*. The world of cabling includes many types of individual cables and cable systems in which connectors and other devices are combined with the cables.

When you plan a network, you're faced with cabling decisions fraught with high initial costs and long-term importance. In Chapter 3, we'll advise you on how to use national and international standards to select the right cables for your installation. In this chapter, we will define some cable buzz words for you and discuss the categories of cables. We'll start with copper cables that carry electrical signals and then move to glass cables that carry pulses of light.

■ Keeping Things In, Keeping Things Out

In networks, the primary job of the connecting cable is to carry the signal from node to node with as little degradation as possible. However, the electrical signal is under constant attack from inside and out. Inside the cable, signals degrade because of various electrical characteristics, including opposition to the flow of electrons, called *resistance*, and opposition to changes in voltage and current, called *reactance*. Electrical impulses from many sources such as lighting, electrical motors, and radio systems can attack the cable from outside.

Network designers can do only a few practical things to limit signal degradation. The techniques typically involve increasing the size of the conductors and improving the type of insulation. These changes increase the size and cost of the cable faster than they improve its quality, so designers typically specify a cable of good practical quality and then specify limitations on the overall length of the cable between nodes.

Each wire in the cable can act like an antenna, absorbing electrical signals from other wires in the cable and from sources of electrical noise outside the cable. The imposed electrical noise can reach such a high level that it becomes difficult for the network interface cards to discriminate between the electrical noise and the desired signal. Electrical noise arising from signals on other wires in the cable is known as *crosstalk*. The potential level of crosstalk is a major limiting factor in the use of some types of cables.

Outside sources of potential interference include radio transmitters, electrical relays and switches, thermostats, and fluorescent lights. This type of interference is commonly referred to as *EMI/RFI noise* (electromagnetic interference/radio frequency interference).

Cable designers use two techniques to protect each wire from undesirable signals: *shielding* and *cancellation*. Shielding is a brute force technique. In a shielded cable, each wire pair or group of wire pairs is surrounded by a metal braid or foil, which acts as a barrier to the interfering signals. Of course, the braid or foil covering increases the diameter of each cable and its cost.

Cancellation is a more elegant approach than shielding. As Figure 2.1 shows, current flowing through a wire creates a small, circular electromagnetic field around the wire. The direction of the current flow in the wire determines the direction of the electromagnetic lines of force encircling the wire. If two wires are in the same electrical circuit, the electrons flow from the negative voltage source to the destination (called a load) in one wire and from the load to the positive source in the other wire. If the two wires are in close proximity, their electromagnetic fields are the exact opposite of each other and cancel out each other and any outside fields as well. Engineers enhance this cancellation effect by twisting the wires. Cancellation is a very effective method of providing self-shielding for wire pairs within a cable.

Figure 2.1

Current flowing through a wire creates an electromagnetic field around the wire. Since the current flows in opposite directions within each wire in an active electrical circuit, the two fields rotate in opposite directions, cancel each other out, and also cancel outside sources of electrical noise. In addition, twisting the two wires together strengthens the fields' ability to resist outside noise.

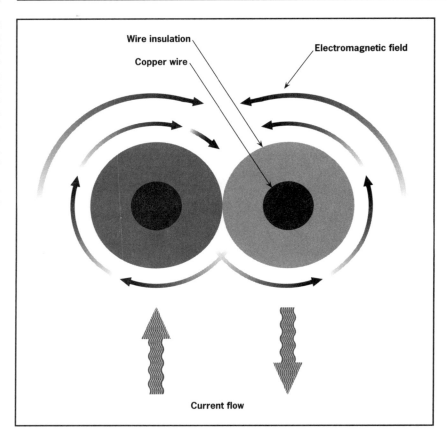

All network cables use one or both of these shielding and cancellation techniques to protect their data. On the bottom line, cables vary in their size, cost, and difficulty of installation primarily because of differences in the shielding and cancellation techniques they use.

HINT. *Problems arise in network installations when the shielding or cancellation protection designed into the cable doesn't carry through into the connectors, patch panels, and interconnection equipment. Poor installation techniques and equipment selection can render all the shielding and cancellation in the cable useless.*

We have briefly described resistance and reactance, but you'll hear the word *impedance* more frequently. Impedance is a complex electrical characteristic involving resistance and reactance, which can only be measured with sophisticated equipment. Cables must have a specific impedance in order to

match the electrical components in the interface cards. A high or low impedance is not good or bad in itself, but a cable must have the correct impedance
to avoid signal loss and interference. The distance between two conductors,
the type of insulation, and other factors determine a specific electrical impedance for each type of cable. Impedance is measured in units called ohms,
which confuses some people because resistance, a less complex electrical
characteristic that is easy to measure with an inexpensive meter, is also measured in ohms. Don't confuse the resistance of a connection or circuit with
the impedance of a cable. Resistance is only one factor in determining impedance. The two factors are slightly interrelated, but they aren't the same, even
though we express them both in ohms.

HINT. *You can't measure the impedance of a cable with an ohm meter. The
common ohm meter only measures electrical resistance. Beware of installers
who don't understand the difference.*

Another seemingly less technical word we'll use is *cable jacket*. The
jacket is the outside covering of the cable—typically some form of plastic,
Teflon, or composite material. The concept is simple, but as we'll describe in
Chapter 3, the jacket on all cable is subject to several complex codes and
regulations. Cables differ in ways that are even more subtle than their size,
weight, and cost. The chemical composition of the materials in the cable,
their spacing, and other factors all have an impact on cable performance.

■ Coaxial Cable

In Chapter 1, we associated the Ethernet networking architecture with coaxial cable. Coaxial cable consists of a center copper conductor (either solid
wire or stranded, but solid is recommended for networks), a layer of flexible
insulation, a shield of woven copper braid or metallic foil, and an outer cable
jacket. The term "coaxial" arose from the fact that the shielding braid and
the center conductor both have the same axis.

The outer braid of coaxial cable makes up one-half of the electrical circuit, in addition to acting as shielding for the inner conductor, so the braid
must make a solid electrical connection at both ends of the cable. Poor shield
connection is the biggest source of connection problems in a coaxial cable installation. (Later, we'll describe other types of shielded wire in which the
shielding is not a part of the circuit.) The cable jacket adds a final layer of insulation and protective coating and completes the package.

Figure 2.2 details the components of a coaxial cable. The coaxial cable
used in thin Ethernet and ARCnet networks has an outside diameter of
about 0.18 inch or 4.7 mm. A larger diameter of coaxial cable is specified for
Ethernet backbone cables. This cable, stiff with shielding and carrying an

easily identified yellow jacket, is often referred to as "frozen yellow garden hose." The Ethernet backbone cable has an outside diameter of approximately 0.4 inch or 9.8 mm.

Figure 2.2

Coaxial cable uses copper shielding to resist interference from outside electrical sources. A braided copper shield surrounds the center conductor and constitutes one-half of the electrical circuit. In some other types of shielded wire, the outer shield is not part of the circuit.

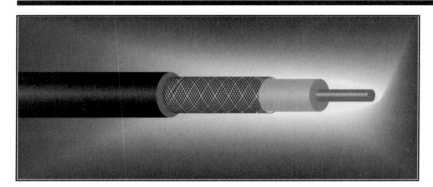

Some LAN signaling schemes, such as Ethernet and ARCnet, depend on coaxial cables with specific impedances that are not interchangeable. Thin Ethernet uses a cable originally described as RG-58, which has an impedance of 52 ohms. Some manufacturers now market for Ethernet use a cable that they describe as 802.3 cable, because it conforms to the standards established by the IEEE 802.3 Committee. ARCnet was originally designed for RG-62 coaxial cable, which has an impedance of 93 ohms. This cable is also used in IBM mainframe computer installations to link IBM 3270 terminals to their controllers. RG-58 and RG-62 cables often look very similar, and sometimes the only way to tell the difference is by reading the labels on the outside of the cable. You'll find RG-59 coaxial cable, with an impedance of 75 ohms, used for cable television wiring in many buildings, but it isn't suitable for any modern networking connections.

Coaxial cable plays an important role in both the ARCnet and Ethernet network architectures, but there is no provision for coaxial cable in token-ring. Originally, ARCnet plans specified that coaxial cable should be installed in a star-shaped configuration—each node had a separate run of coaxial cable going to a central wiring hub. This configuration reduces the chance that one bad cable segment might bring down the entire network. Some companies later introduced ARCnet network adapters that allow different cable configurations, but star wiring with coaxial cable and hubs remains the most popular arrangement.

Originally, the Ethernet scheme allowed for a plan called "thin Ethernet" using the RG-58 type cable arranged in a node-to-node or daisy-chain wiring scheme. In this configuration, one break in the cable or one bad connector could disrupt the entire network. Manufacturers of wiring hubs now market connectors for coaxial cable that allow you to configure thin Ethernet in a star-wired arrangement with separate lengths of coax running between each node and the wiring hub. This arrangement is particularly useful wherever high electrical noise is a problem. A star-wired thin Ethernet arrangement combines the excellent shielding capabilities of coax with the highly reliable star-wiring scheme.

Despite its benefits, the networking industry is moving away from coaxial cable. However, we still recommend it for its reliability, particularly in a star-wired configuration, but new developments and standards are moving toward unshielded twisted-pair wire.

■ Unshielded Twisted Pair (UTP)

As the name implies, twisted-pair cable is composed of pairs of wires; each pair is insulated from each other and twisted together within an outer jacket. There is no physical shielding on UTP cable; it derives all of its protection from the cancellation effect of the twisted-wire pairs. The mutual cancellation effect reduces crosstalk between pairs and EMI/RFI noise. Network designers vary the number of twists in the different wire pairs within each cable to reduce the electrical coupling and crosstalk between the pairs. UTP cable relies solely on this cancellation effect to minimize the absorption and radiation of electrical energy.

Unshielded twisted-pair cable designed for networks, shown in Figure 2.3, contains four pairs of 22- or 24-gauge solid copper wires. The cable has an impedance of 100 ohms—an important factor that differentiates it from other types of twisted-pair and telephone wiring. Network UTP cable has an external diameter of about 0.17 inch or 4.3 mm. This small size is advantageous during installation.

HINT. *In American Wire Gauge (AWG) standards, larger numbers indicate smaller wires. Other standards, described in Chapter 3, will guide your cable purchase, but beware of any cabling in your installation that uses wires which look too thin or are stranded instead of solid.*

UTP continues to grow in popularity. You can use UTP with each of the three major networking architectures (ARCnet, Ethernet, and token-ring), although in some cases the wire pairs appear on different pin connections in the wall jacks. In most cases, you must order network interface cards for the specific type of cabling, but many Ethernet interface cards come configured for both coaxial cable and UTP.

Figure 2.3

Unshielded twisted-pair cable (UTP) for networks uses four pairs of wire in the same jacket. Each wire pair has a different degree of twisting to reduce the coupling and crosstalk between them.

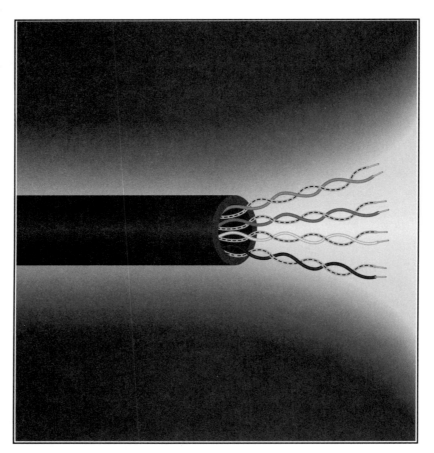

UTP's Pluses and Minuses

While UTP is popular, some of its potential and often highly lauded advantages, such as ease of installation and low cost, don't survive close scrutiny. Certainly it requires less training and equipment to install UTP than it does to install fiber-optic cable, but it still takes a great deal of care and skill to install a UTP system capable of reliably carrying data moving at the token-ring signaling 10 or 16 megabits per second. Newer standards call for using UTP at 100 megabits per second, but these cable plants will have to be carefully planned and installed. (You'll learn more about signaling rates in Chapter 4.)

It's true that UTP costs less per foot than any other type of LAN cabling, but materials are the least significant cost of any installation, with labor typically costing the most. Many people trained in UTP installation are available, due to the prevalence of UTP in the telephone industry. However, the cable television industry has created a pool of people with coaxial cable and fiber-optic installation skills, so the cost of the labor for those types of installations is declining.

On the bottom line, UTP's real advantage is its size. UTP doesn't fill wiring ducts as quickly as other cable types (it's about the same size as fiber-optic cable). In an existing building, its small size makes pulling UTP through the walls easier. In a new building, wiring with UTP makes it possible to plan for more connections without seriously diminishing vital utility space.

Telephone Wire ≠ LAN Cable

Many people confuse UTP wire designed for network data with the telephone wire already installed in their walls. They are seldom the same. The telephone wiring in use in most residences is called *quad*. Quad has four non-twisted parallel wires in one cable. Silver satin is another type of telephone wire found in some modern buildings. Silver satin cable is flat and typically has a silver-colored vinyl jacket. In older buildings, you'll often find thick multiconductor cables designed for a type of telephone system called a key system. None of these wiring systems—quad, silver satin, or key system—is adequate for modern LAN data services. Figure 2.4 shows you what types of cable to avoid.

Even though some digital telephone private branch exchange (PBX) systems do use high quality, shielded twisted-pair wire, it typically isn't installed in the same pair configuration called for in local area networks. Even a sophisticated digital PBX wiring plant can require a great deal of modification before it can be used for ARCnet, Ethernet, or token-ring networking. Even if they do have the correct type of wire, existing wiring plants often exhibit problems when you try to use them to carry high-speed data. If you are going to bet your business on your network, you should probably plan on installing a new LAN wiring system.

Older cable plants often suffer from out-of-date documentation, so you don't know which cables go where or, most importantly, their length. Standard PBX wiring installations provide four pairs of wires to the wall jack; two pairs are used by the PBX telephone system and two pairs might be free. However, if you have an intercom or other special telephone feature, all of your pairs will be used. Also, a rule of thumb is that 2 to 3 percent of wire pairs in an installation are bad. When the number of available pairs is already marginal, attrition takes a big toll. The cost of testing an existing cable plant, troubleshooting, and making modifications to meet current standards often offsets the cost of pulling new cable.

Figure 2.4

Although you might already find them in the walls of your building, these cables are not network cables. They don't conform to the electrical specifications for LAN adapters and won't reliably carry LAN signals over practical distances.

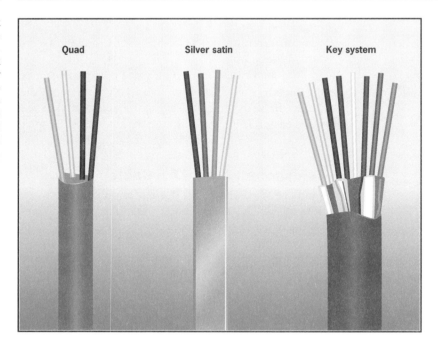

Despite the questionable benefits of some of its so-called advantages, UTP is secure in its growing dominance of the network cable industry. Much of this book focuses on the selection and installation of UTP, but in later chapters, you'll see how coaxial, shielded twisted-pair, and fiber-optic cable each can solve specific networking problems.

■ Shielded Twisted Pair (STP)

Shielded twisted pair (STP), as the name implies, combines both shielding and cancellation techniques. STP cable designed for networking comes in two varieties. The simplest STP is called "100 ohm shielded" because, like UTP, it has a 100 ohm impedance and has an added shield of copper braid around all the wire pairs. But the most common form of STP, introduced by IBM and associated with the IEEE 802.5 token-ring networking architecture, is known as 150 ohm STP because of its 150 ohm impedance. Figure 2.5 illustrates 150 ohm shielded twisted-pair wire.

The style of STP cable introduced by IBM for Token-Ring uses a "belt and suspenders" approach to engineering. Not only is the entire 150 STP cable shielded to reduce EMI/RFI, but each pair of twisted wires is shielded from each other by a separate shield to reduce crosstalk. In addition, each pair is twisted to benefit from the effects of cancellation. Note that unlike co-axial cable, the shielding on 150 ohm STP isn't part of the signal path, but is grounded at both ends.

Figure 2.5

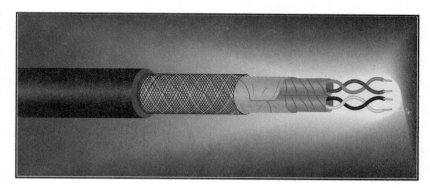

The shielded twisted-pair wire used in IBM's Token-Ring networking system shields each pair of wires individually to reduce crosstalk and then shields the entire cable to reduce outside interference. This conservative approach provides an excellent electrical environment, but the cable has a large outside diameter and is expensive.

On the positive side, 150 ohm STP can carry data using very fast signaling with little chance of distortion. On the negative side, all of the shielding causes signal loss that increases the need for greater spacing (that is, more insulation) between the wire pairs and the shield. The increased amount of insulation and the large amount of shielding considerably increases the size, weight, and cost of the cable. IBM-style STP, with an outside diameter of approximately 0.4 inch or 0.98 mm, quickly fills wiring ducts. Wiring a building for IBM Token-Ring with STP requires the installation of large wiring closets and large wiring ducts.

The 100 ohm STP, used primarily for Ethernet installations, improves the EMI/RFI resistance of twisted-pair wire without a significant gain in size or weight. The shield is not part of the data circuit, so it is only grounded at one end—typically at the wiring closet or hub. However, properly grounding the shield on the cable isn't easy, particularly if you want to make use of older wiring hubs that aren't designed for STP. If it isn't grounded at one end, the shield becomes an antenna and your problems multiply.

Mod-Tap and other companies market patch panels that can grasp the cable shield and ground it. You can terminate all of the 100 ohm shielded twisted-pair cables in the patch panel and retain the wiring hub and LAN adapters you've already installed, but you'll need a good ground connection for the patch panel. 100 ohm shielded twisted-pair cable offers more protection from interference than unshielded twisted-pair. It also maintains compatibility with 10Base-T wiring hubs and avoids the conduit crowding problems of 150 ohm shielded twisted-pair wire.

■ Fiber-optic Cable

Whereas copper wires carry electrons, fiber-optic cables made of glass fibers carry light. The advantages of fiber include complete immunity from crosstalk and EMI/RFI. The lack of internal and external noise means that signals go farther and can move faster, which translates to both greater speed and distance than copper cabling. Since fiber can't carry electrical power, it is the perfect medium to connect buildings that might have different electrical grounds. Also, the long cable spans between buildings can't serve as an entry point for lightning like they can if the inter-building links are copper cables. Finally, a two-fiber cable, in which each fiber carries a beam of light in one direction, is about the same size as UTP: approximately 0.21 inch or 5.3 mm. Because it is flat like a piece of lamp cord, you can get many fiber cables in a single conduit.

If fiber-optic cable offers so many benefits, why do we still use copper? The answer lies in interface devices and the cost of connections. As an optical interface, a fiber-optic connector must make a precise right angle and polished connection to the end of the strand, which clearly makes installation more difficult. Installers typically attend a one-day training course, but the only way to learn is through practice, and each practice connection can cost eight to ten dollars, so the course is a costly investment in training. It takes a trained installer several minutes to make a connection, so the hourly cost of labor is high in a large installation, and the installer needs an expensive toolkit to make even one connection.

Finally, the fiber-optic transceivers at each end of the cable are expensive. A fiber-optic LAN card costs five to seven times as much as an Ethernet card for copper cable. So, while fiber is alluring, it is difficult to justify the cost of running fiber to each desktop. In modern installations, fiber makes up the backbone between wiring hubs and between buildings. Fiber interfaces are available for all ARCnet, Ethernet, and token-ring wiring hubs.

Fiber-optic communication has its roots in 19th-century inventions. A device called the Photophen converted voice signals into optical signals using sunlight and lenses mounted on a transducer that vibrated to the sound. Fiber optics became practical in the 1960s with the introduction of solid state light sources—lasers and light-emitting diodes—and high quality glass free of most impurities. Telephone companies pioneered fiber-optic techniques to gain all of its benefits for long distance connections.

A typical fiber-optic LAN cable, shown in Figure 2.6, has two fibers that terminate in two separate connectors. Some cables combine fibers and twisted copper inside the same jacket, and cables with multiple fibers are common, but the link between a node and a cable hub is always made using two fibers, each of which carries light in one direction.

Figure 2.6

A fiber-optic cable for networks consists of two fibers in separate sheaths. Each glass fiber is surrounded by reflective cladding, a plastic coating, a protective layer of Kevlar, and an outer jacket.

Each half of the fiber optic cable is composed of layers of material. On the outside, a plastic jacket that must conform to the appropriate fire and building codes for the installation protects that entire cable. Under the jacket, a layer of Kevlar fibers (also used in bulletproof vests) provides cushioning and strength. Under the Kevlar, another layer of plastic, called the *coating*, typically adds cushioning and protection. Some fiber-optic cables designed for burial might include a stainless steel wire or other materials for added strength. All of these materials protect the hair-thin glass strand.

The center of each glass strand, called the *core*, is where the data actually travels. Light from a diode or laser enters the core at one end and is trapped by the shiny walls of the core—a phenomenon called *total internal reflection*. The size of the core is measured in microns. Two standard sizes for the core are 62.5 and 100 microns, equal to about 0.002 inch.

WARNING. *Never look directly into an unmarked optical cable to determine if it is fiber-optic cable. Permanent eye damage may result, because the light that moves through the cable is often intense but not visible to the human eye.*

The core is surrounded by a glass or plastic coating, called the *cladding,* that has a different optical density than the core. The boundary between the cladding and the core reflects the light back into the core. Cladding typically is 125 or 140 microns thick—about 0.003 inch.

In later chapters we'll provide more details about the selection and use of fiber-optic cable, but for now you should understand that it is economical for specific applications such as connecting wiring centers. Additionally, fiber is highly recommended for some applications, such as connecting separate buildings, but running fiber to every desktop is an expensive alternative.

■ Making Decisions

Many network designers focus on decisions such as what brand of network operating system to use or what kind of server hardware to buy. But in many installations, selecting the cable is the first major step in network design. Final decisions about software and computer hardware can wait, but the early actions of architects and construction crews hinge on the cable decision.

We suggest that you consider the following factors when making your cable decision:

- What is the present need for signaling speed? What do the applications require?

- Can you foresee future needs for signaling speed? Are high-density graphics on the horizon?

- Are you required to comply with building and fire codes? Do you have cable conduit space? Architectural considerations? Local building code restrictions?

Once you understand those factors, then decide:

- Do you want to rely on copper or fiber? How widely dispersed are the nodes? What can you afford? Is this a backbone or a lobe to a LAN node?

- Which will better suit your network, twisted-pair or coaxial cable? Do you have an existing investment in either type of cable?

- If you opt for twisted-pair cable, should you get shielded or unshielded? Does your noisy electrical environment dictate a need for shielded cable?

Each of these decisions leads you into a different area of standards and specifications. In the following chapters we'll provide more detailed information to guide your decisions and installation techniques.

- *Who Said So?*
- *Company Plans*
- *National Electrical Code (NEC)*
- *The EIA/TIA-568 Standard*
- *Underwriters Laboratories (UL)*
- *Evolution*

3

Standards: There Are So Many!

"Willy, I need help. I've got to put together a specification for this network and I don't know where to start."

The center of focus of Willy's desk was a bottomless tray of paperwork, so any distraction, even one from a blustery high school principal, was welcome. He cleaned off a chair so the young woman could sit down, "Let me get this straight, Sara, you want me to help you write a wide-open specification for the high school network so that anybody, including me, can bid on it?"

"Yeah, who else in town could write it so it is both fair and technically correct?" the principal replied.

"But you will let me bid on it?"

"Sure, we'll invite a round of comments before the final bid, and, if you've snuck anything in that locks up the job for you, we'll hold a public lynching," she quipped with a straight face.

"You do know that every electrical contractor in four counties will try to bid? Most of them don't know anything about data systems, but they'll all claim they can pull wire. Are you ready for the screams when they can't bid because of the technical specifications?"

The principal was a realist who worked for an elected superintendent of schools. She weighed the political consequences before speaking. "Have you got some technical stuff we can put in there that's rock solid and supported by the federal government or something?"

"The best. You probably have county or state rules forcing you to buy only UL marked products anyway." Willy fished in a desk drawer and pulled out a thin pamphlet with the title: "UL's LAN Cable Certification Program." "Anybody can get this pamphlet. It doesn't tell you how to install the cable, but it does describe the technical specifications for the cable. If we ask for the UL Level IV marking in your request for bids, you'll get the correct cable no matter who wins.

"But," Willy continued, "there's still a problem. Getting the right grade of cable is only a small part of the job. If the cable isn't properly installed, the network might work inefficiently because the LAN adapters have to resend data, or it might not work when you move to higher speeds in a few years. So, we're going to ask the installer to provide a report, on paper, showing the crosstalk and attenuation on every cable span. That report does two things: It insures that the installation is done right the first time, and it gives you an excellent place to start troubleshooting problems in the future. It also cuts out the people who don't know crosstalk from a crosswalk."

Willy was still hesitant about getting too involved with creating the statement of requirements for a job he wanted to bid on. So he sent the principal back to school armed with the UL pamphlet and a sample crosstalk and attenuation report. Willy gave Sara one piece of advice as he walked her to the door: "Your network is never any better than the cabling, Sara. Don't limit your network's capability tomorrow by making short-sighted cabling decisions today."

Both the value and the wonder of today's networks are that many different products from many different companies all work together. A LAN adapter from 3Com and a LAN adapter from Standard Microsystems communicate with each other across a network cable because the designers of both adapters followed the same standards for interaction across the cable.

As Figure 3.1 shows, a hierarchy of standards controls the interface to the application programs, the actions of network communications programs, the design of LAN adapters, the cable connectors, and the cables themselves. In the example in this figure, the Windows Open Systems Architecture (WOSA) tells programmers how to write programs that can access the services available within the Microsoft Windows environment. The File Transfer Protocol (FTP) from the TCP/IP standards, Microsoft's Server Message Block (SMB), and the IBM NetBIOS protocol all provide different ways for programs to communicate across a network. The Internet Protocol (IP) and Internetwork Packet Exchange (IPX) protocol define how networking software carries data from node to node. The IEEE 802 family of specifications is used to design network interface cards. But the cable itself is governed by a confusing mix of standards ranging from fire codes to detailed electrical specifications and tests for safety and performance.

Unfortunately, the specifications and standards for cables having evolved from many sources, and are often overlapping and confusing.

In this chapter, we examine some important cable plant standards and we explain the designations and specifications you'll find useful when you write a request for proposal or make a purchase. But using the right materials doesn't insure that an installation will meet the performance specification. Many factors determine the quality of the total installation, including

- How much the wire is untwisted before it reaches a termination

- The type of termination equipment

- The electrical noise in various frequency bands

- The near-end crosstalk (NEXT) caused by wires in proximity to each other

You can get a good start on a high quality installation by using the correct cable. However, this alone does not guarantee a good installation because the actions of the installer are critical to the overall quality of your cable plant.

This chapter deals primarily with specifications that apply to shielded and unshielded twisted-pair wire. The "Company Plans" section will unravel this twisted bundle of terms by looking at the plans and specifications developed by specific companies.

Figure 3.1

Modern networks
function according to
openly published
standards supported by
many companies.

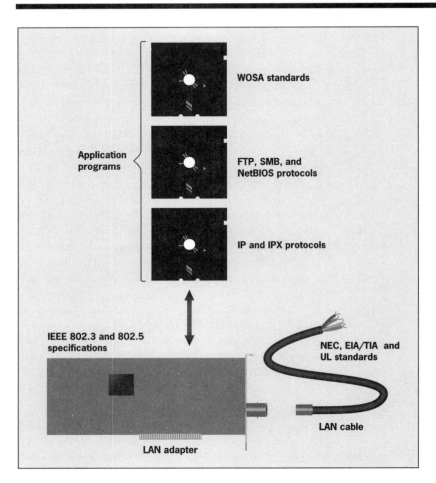

■ Who Said So?

Numerous companies, organizations, and even government bodies regulate and specify the cables you use. Some companies, such as AT&T, Digital Equipment Corporation, Hewlett-Packard, IBM, and Northern Telecom, have volumes of detailed specifications that go beyond the cable to include the connectors, wiring and distribution centers, and installation techniques. These plans are called premises distribution systems (PDSs), and we described a generic PDS in Chapter 2. We'll describe the pros and cons of these company-specific PDS architectures later in this chapter.

National and international organizations that develop fire and building codes, such as

- The Institute of Electrical and Electronic Engineers (IEEE)

- The Electronic Industries Association and the newer Telecommunications Industry Association (EIA/TIA)

- Underwriters Laboratories (UL)

- Government agencies at various levels

all issue specifications for cable material and installation. EIA/TIA has issued EIA/TIA-568 and -569 standards for technical performance, and has an active program to extend its requirements. (See "The EIA/TIA-568 Standard" section later in this chapter.) The IEEE has included minimal cable requirements in its 802.3 and 802.5 specifications for Ethernet and Token-Ring systems. Because the IEEE 802.3 and 802.5 standards focus as much on network access as on cabling, we'll describe them in Chapter 4.

The National Electrical Code of the United States (NEC) describes various types of cables and materials used in the cable. The UL focuses on safety standards, but has expanded its certification program to evaluate twisted-pair LAN cables for performance according to IBM and EIA/TIA performance specifications as well as NEC safety specifications. The UL also established a program to mark shielded and unshielded twisted-pair LAN cables that should simplify the complex task of making sure the materials used in the installation are up to specification.

As we explained in Chapter 2, the designations for coaxial cable had the benefit of being set in practice before most of the standards committees began their deliberations. (The chart in Chapter 2 describes the typical coaxial cables and their different impedance ratings.) In Chapter 4, we describe the associations between specific types of coaxial cable and local area network architectures.

■ Company Plans

AT&T, Digital Equipment Corporation, IBM, and Northern Telecom, along with other companies, have developed and published complete architectures for structured cabling systems called premises distribution systems (PDSs). AT&T calls its architecture the AT&T Systimax Premises Distribution System; Digital uses the name Open DECconnect; IBM calls its architecture simply the IBM Cabling System; and Northern Telecom has the Integrated Building Distribution Network (IBDN). IBM and AT&T fielded their systems in 1984 and 1985 and DECconnect came out in 1986. Northern Telecom's

IBDN, which is quite similar to AT&T's Systimax, is a relative newcomer that emerged in 1991.

Overall, the plans from IBM and AT&T have had the most profound effect on the cabling industry. You'll often see cables in catalogs rated in terms of IBM or AT&T specifications. IBM's concept of cable *types* permeates the industry, while AT&T has influenced every cable and connector standard.

Other companies, particularly Amp, Inc., Anixter, and Mod-Tap, market and sell specific equipment for structured cabling systems. Anixter especially deserves praise for setting openly documented and fair performance and electrical standards for twisted-pair wiring. Anixter's original concept of *levels* is used by EIA/TIA and UL in their standards.

IBM Cabling System

Interestingly, IBM does not sell the cables or connectors they describe in their documentation. IBM's goal in creating and supporting the IBM Cabling Plan is to have a stable and known environment for the operation of its computer equipment. You can buy cables and parts certified to meet the IBM specifications from a variety of vendors, and you can find local contractors who will install the PDS according to IBM's specifications.

HINT. *If you're installing an IBM network, ask prospective installers which IBM schools their employees have attended and what experience they have in following the IBM Cabling Plan specifications. As a rule, it doesn't pay to let a vendor learn on your installation.*

The heart of the IBM cabling system is a series of specifications for wire types. The IBM architecture contains the only significant support in the industry for shielded twisted-pair wire. STP, specified in IBM's Type 1, Type 2, Type 6, Type 8, and Type 9 cable, described below, replaces the older RG-62 coaxial cable IBM used to use to link terminals to mainframe computers under the IBM 3270 terminal plan. STP is the wiring alternative IBM recommends for both 4 and 16 megabit-per-second Token-Ring installations. The IBM Cabling Plan also uses fiber-optic cable (see Chapter 8 for more information) and unshielded twisted-pair wire, but the heart of the system is shielded twisted-pair wire. Here is a brief description of the IBM wire types:

- Type 1 cable consists of shielded cable with two twisted pairs made from 22 AWG solid wire (as opposed to the stranded wire in Type 6, below). Used for data transmission, particularly with Token-Ring networks, the cable has an impedance of 150 ohms. Each pair of wires has its own shielding and then the entire cable is shielded by an external braid. Type 1 cable is tested to a bandwidth of 100 MHz and has a data transmission rating of 100 megabits per second. See Figure 3.2 and the discussion of the EIA/TIA-568 Category 5 and the UL Level V later in this chapter.

Figure 3.2

Many companies sell
cable that follows IBM's
Type 1 specification. This
cable combines two
separately shielded pairs
of solid twisted wire. PVC
and Teflon jackets
provide different degrees
of fire resistance.

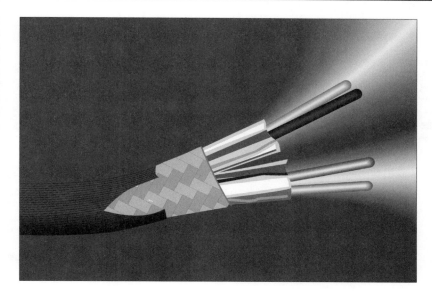

IBM has added a new specification that uses the same cable but subjects it to more rigorous testing. This specification, called Type 1A, calls for cable tested to 300 MHz and has applications in areas requiring very high-speed data, such as Asynchronous Transfer Mode communications (ATM).

- Type 2 cable consists of unshielded pairs of 22 AWG solid wire for voice telephone and two shielded data pairs meeting the Type 1 specification in the same sheath. Type 2 was originally designed to provide voice and data transmission in the same cable. See Type 3 cable below for more information on the unshielded twisted pairs in the Type 2 cable. A new Type 2A, with the same configuration but tested to 600 MHz, is also available. See Figure 3.3.

- Type 3 cable consists of four unshielded 24 AWG solid twisted pairs for voice or data with a characteristic impedance of 105 ohms. Type 3 is IBM's version of twisted-pair telephone wire. The unshielded pairs in Type 2 cable and Type 3 cable are designed only for telephone and low-speed data transmission of up to 4 megabits per second and do not meet the requirements for higher-speed data transmission. Do not confuse IBM Type 3 cable with EIA/TIA 568 Category 3 or UL Level III cable described later in this chapter; it looks similar, but it is not the same.

- Type 4 cable lacks a published specification.

Figure 3.3

Cables that follow IBM's Type 2 cable specifications are used primarily to combine telephone and Token-Ring wiring within the same cable installation. Two pairs of shielded twisted-pair wires are joined with four unshielded twisted pairs within the same outer jacket.

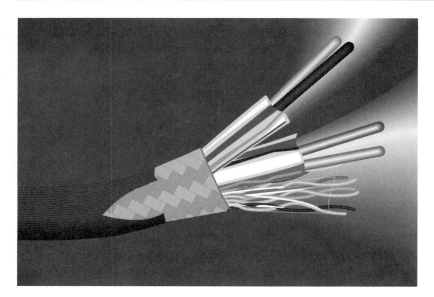

- Type 5 cable consists of two fiber-optic strands. This cable has a 100 micron core and measures 140 microns with cladding. It has a window at 850 nm and a bandwidth of 100 MHz. Note that Type 5 cable differs considerably from the more popular 62.5/125 micron dual-window fiber-optic cable. Type 5 is accepted as part of the Fiber Distributed Data Interface (FDDI) specification, but the 62.5/125 micron cable, also part of the FDDI specification, is more common.

- Type 6 cable consists of shielded cable with two twisted pairs made from 26 AWG stranded wire. More flexible than Type 1 cable, and designed for data transmission, Type 6 is commonly used between a computer and a data jack in the wall. A Type 6A, tested to 600 MHz, is also available.

- Type 7 cable lacks a published specification.

- Type 8 cable is a special "under-the-carpet," shielded twisted-pair cable designed to minimize the lump in the carpet that covers it. This cable contains two parallel untwisted pairs of 23 AWG solid conductors and has little practical use in modern data installations.

- Type 9 cable is plenum cable. It consists of two individually shielded twisted pairs of 26 AWG solid or stranded copper wire, covered with a special flame-retardant coating, for use between floors in a building. A Type 9A, tested to 600 MHz, is also available.

NOTE. *When you hear or read references to Type 1 cable, you should immediately think of shielded twisted-pair wiring, but note that many speakers and writers don't clearly differentiate between the IBM cable types and often really mean Type 2 or Type 6 cable.*

The primary advantage of IBM's Cable Plan is in its conservative engineering. IBM not only relies on heavy shielding around all the pairs to keep electrical noise out, but specifies shielding between both the pairs and the twistings to keep down the crosstalk between the pairs. This is belt-and-suspenders engineering. The specifications keep wiring runs short to avoid problems caused by the degrading of the signals with distance. If the installer follows the plan, the cable system will work in practically any electrical environment, and be viable well beyond the life of the computer equipment in the installation.

The primary drawback to the IBM Cable Plan is the heaviness and bulk of the shielded twisted-pair cable. Type 1 cable, with an outside diameter of between .32 and .5 inch, depending on the manufacturer and the type of outside jacket, quickly fills wiring conduits and cascades into wiring closets in a huge waterfall of cable.

Another significant drawback to the IBM plan is the cost of the cabling and the connectors. On a per-foot basis, Type 1 cable costs approximately four times as much as the highest quality unshielded twisted-pair wire designed for the same conditions. The IBM Data Connector, shown in Figure 3.4, costs about 16 times the price of an RJ-45 connector, typically used on unshielded twisted-pair wire, and has about that same ratio of size. So while it might be good, IBM's cable plan is bulky and expensive.

AT&T Systimax

AT&T's Systimax is deeply rooted in history. Before the breakup of the Bell System in the United States, the technical side of the telephone industry was controlled by a series of publications called the Bell Standard Practices (BSPs). Because it was largely a monopoly, the telephone industry didn't need many standards beyond those in the BSPs. The BSPs described in detail how installers should cut, twist, and attach every wire, and how to secure every cable span. The Systimax specifications are at least spiritual and cultural offspring of the BSPs. They are detailed and, if followed, can give you a flexible, reliable, and expandable cable plant.

AT&T manufactures, sells, and installs the products in the Systimax family. The company also provides training, so you will find many installers in local companies who know how to work to Systimax specifications. The IBM Cabling Plan is built on shielded twisted-pair wiring, but the AT&T Systimax is based on unshielded twisted-pair wire for horizontal wiring and fiber-optic cabling for everything else. While it takes about 3 inches of AT&T catalogs to describe all of the products in the Systimax line, the next four sections cover a few of the key elements.

Figure 3.4

The IBM Data Connector is versatile, relatively easy to install, large, and expensive. This connector typically plugs into a Token-Ring wiring hub (MAU in IBM terminology) and has a dust cap. Interestingly, two identical connectors can plug together to create a cable extension.

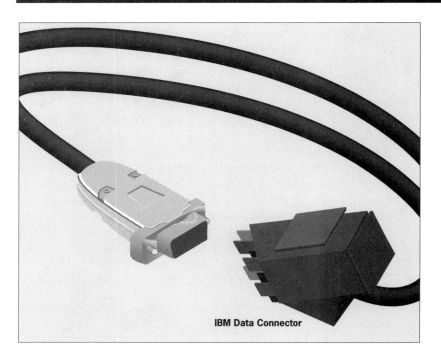

IBM Data Connector

AT&T offers five-year assurance programs for Systimax components installed by AT&T value-added resellers. This warranty protects against defects in cable and other products manufactured by AT&T and against the system's becoming obsolete for specified applications. Systimax is a comprehensive and proven premises distribution system that serves as a standard for all installations. Whether you think it's more than you need depends on how much you value your network.

AT&T 1061A and 2061A LAN Cables

The AT&T LAN cables, shown in Figure 3.5, include four pairs of unshielded twisted-pair 24 AWG copper wire in different jackets for non-plenum and plenum installations. This is the Systimax 100 ohm impedance cable for horizontal-wiring data applications. Note that the four-pair cable provides two spare pairs in most installations. With an outside diameter of about .17 inch, this cable is easy to pull through conduits and inside walls. The Systimax specifications allow a cable run of 100 meters for data transmission at speeds of up to 16 megabits per second.

Figure 3.5

AT&T 1061A LAN cable is a good choice for all unshielded twisted-pair data-transmission applications. Each cable contains four unshielded twisted pairs.

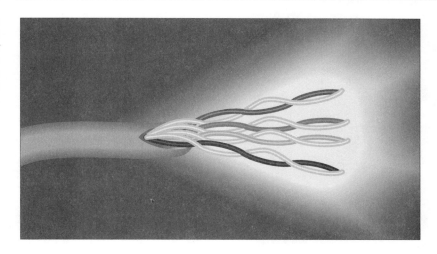

AT&T 1090 and 2290 Cables

This composite cable shown in Figure 3.6, combining copper and fiber-optic conductors, is the ultimate horizontal-wiring choice for people who want to make sure they will never outgrow their cabling systems. It provides a total of eight unshielded twisted pairs—the equivalent of two runs of AT&T 1061A or 2061A cable—and two fibers inside one jacket. This combination provides plenty of bandwidth for data and voice telephone connections to any desktop and the capability to add fiber connections for higher-speed data, video, or other applications. If you have a big budget and plan to own the building forever, we think this is the right cable to install, but, like the IBM Cable Plan, it is expensive and bulky.

Figure 3.6

AT&T 1090 cable combines two fibers with two separate cable runs containing four unshielded twisted pairs. This cable is bulky and expensive, but it provides a desktop with the ultimate in available bandwidth.

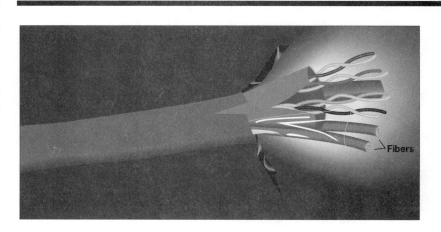

AT&T Accumax

AT&T offers a variety of fiber-optic cables to use as backbone cable to link wiring closets and as horizontal wiring for special applications. Some products in this family group as many as 216 fibers together inside a protective jacket for the long trip up an elevator or air shaft. The AT&T fiber-optic standard calls for 62.5/125 micron multimode fiber with windows at 850 nm and 1300 nm and a bandwidth of 160 MHz and 500 MHz. These fibers have gray jackets. AT&T also offers single-mode fiber cables with yellow jackets.

The 110 Cross-Connect and Patch Panel Systems

The AT&T 110 Connector System includes several types of rack or wall-mounted connector hardware that typically goes into a wiring closet to terminate horizontal and backbone cable. The 110 Cross-Connect System, shown in Figure 3.7, uses jumper wire and punch-down tools to make connections between circuits. The 110 Patch Panel System, shown in Figure 3.8, uses patch cords for more flexibility, but it is more expensive and requires more space than the 110 Cross-Connect System. You can include both types of interconnection systems in your wiring plan to get the best mix of flexibility and economy.

AT&T Plug and Jack Standards

Taking the wiring almost up to the desktop, AT&T offers a variety of outlets that terminate eight conductors for data and voice connections. The wiring sequence for these jacks—which wire goes to which terminal—is critical to the proper operation of the network (see Figure 3.9). AT&T's Standard 258A is the most widely specified wiring sequence for 4-pair plugs and jacks. It is also the same as the wiring sequence specified for Integrated Services Digital Network (ISDN) and 10Base-T Ethernet over unshielded twisted-pair wiring. AT&T Standards 258A and 356A define the sequence used to connect pairs of wires to plugs and jacks. The 356A standard deals with three pairs of wires, but the 258A standard for four pairs of wires is now the most widely specified in the industry. The older USOC code was used in the U.S. Bell telephone system. Note that for pairs 2 through 4, the AT&T 258A sequence is different from the older Universal Service Order Code (USOC) sequence (Figure 3.9), which is used for many voice telephone installations. Confusion over these wire sequences is a major cause of cable plant installation problems. Intermixing USOC and 258A wired plugs and jacks is a sure setting for a variety of problems ranging from no connection to mysteriously poor network performance.

Figure 3.7

The AT&T 110 Cross-Connect System is the modern version of a punch-down block. Using short jumper wires, it provides high-quality interconnections between data circuits.

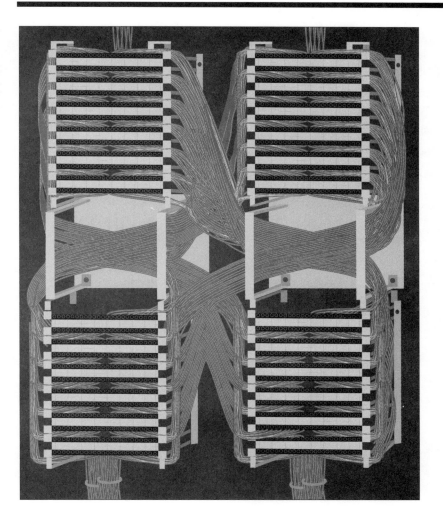

Amp and Mod-Tap

An appendix in this book lists companies that manufacture or sell PDS components. Two companies, Amp and Mod-Tap, stand head and shoulders above their competition in terms of consistently providing quality products, trained installers, and support for their products. These two companies don't attempt to set PDS standards; instead, they make and market cable and connection products that conform to popular standards while also innovating and providing improved convenience and quality.

Figure 3.8

The AT&T 110 Patch Panel System is the standard for patch panels. Amp, Mod-Tap, and Krone make competing systems.

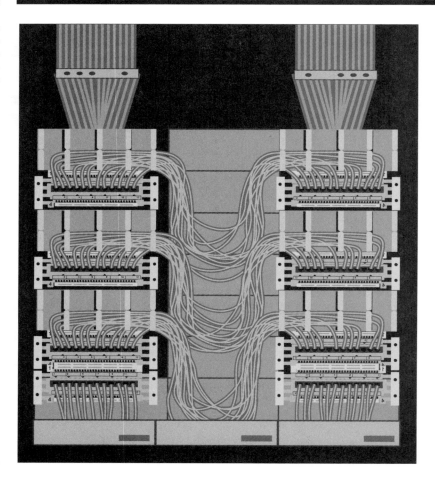

Both AMP and Mod-Tap have training programs for installers. We strongly recommend that you ask your installer for a training history and references.

Amp Products

Amp is well known as a manufacturer of connectors. You probably have Amp connectors on your printer cables and perhaps on high-quality RS-232 serial cables. In the network cabling market, Amp has products for the ends of the cables, the wall plates, the wiring hubs, and the distribution frame.

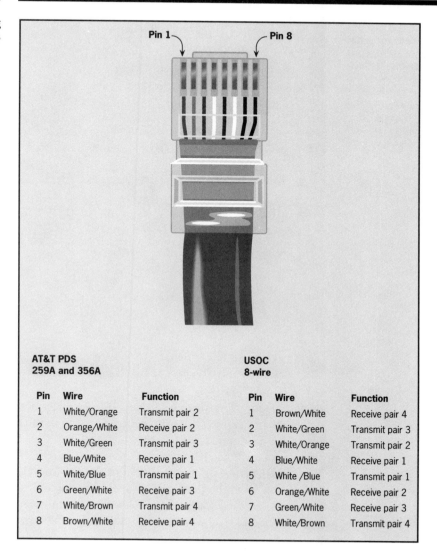

Figure 3.9

AT&T and USOC wiring
standards

Pin 1   Pin 8

AT&T PDS 259A and 356A			USOC 8-wire		
Pin	**Wire**	**Function**	**Pin**	**Wire**	**Function**
1	White/Orange	Transmit pair 2	1	Brown/White	Receive pair 4
2	Orange/White	Receive pair 2	2	White/Green	Transmit pair 3
3	White/Green	Transmit pair 3	3	White/Orange	Transmit pair 2
4	Blue/White	Receive pair 1	4	Blue/White	Receive pair 1
5	White/Blue	Transmit pair 1	5	White /Blue	Transmit pair 1
6	Green/White	Receive pair 3	6	Orange/White	Receive pair 2
7	White/Brown	Transmit pair 4	7	Green/White	Receive pair 3
8	Brown/White	Receive pair 4	8	White/Brown	Transmit pair 4

LAN-Line Thinnet Tap   AMP demonstrated innovation in the design of the LAN-Line Thinnet Tap system, shown in Figure 3.10. This unique wall jack provides an answer to the difficult challenge of making a neat and reliable connection using thin Ethernet coaxial cable. A single physical cable goes from the wall plate to the node, eliminating the possibility of someone's disabling the entire network by disconnecting the cable from a T-connector.

Figure 3.10

Amp's unique LAN-Line Thinnet Tap for thin Ethernet installations significantly reduces potential network cabling problems by eliminating T-connectors. It provides a high-quality single cable connection from the wall plate to the LAN adapter.

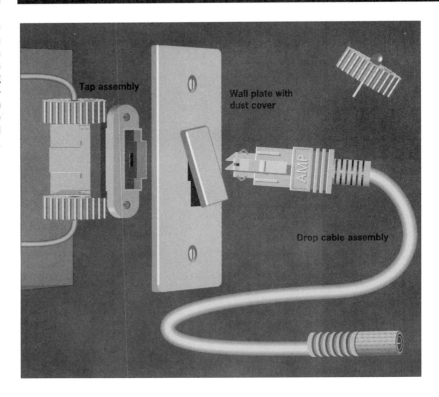

Access Floor Workstation Model   The location of telephone, power, and network connections is a prime consideration in the design of modern offices. But designers can't anticipate all the desk and divider configurations that people will use when they inhabit a building. The Amp Access Floor Workstation Module, shown in Figure 3.11, allows designers to bury a series of connectors in the floor until they're needed. Until someone places a desk by the Floor Workstation Module, it lies flat and matches the floor covering. When it's needed, the system can be configured with a variety of connectors.

AMPIX Cross-Connect System   Among its many products, Amp markets a Cross-Connect distribution system for voice and data, with specially designed, high-quality wire terminations and printed-circuit-board connections between the wire termination and the RJ-45 jack of the patch-board system. Figure 3.12 shows an Amp modular-jack field with Amp barrel terminals for the wires. Amp also has a wide variety of fiber-optic-cable splicing, terminating, and testing equipment.

Figure 3.11

The Amp Access Floor Workstation Module provides a standardized method of prepositioning power, telephone, and network connections within a building. You can change the connectors within the module to meet the needs of the particular worker.

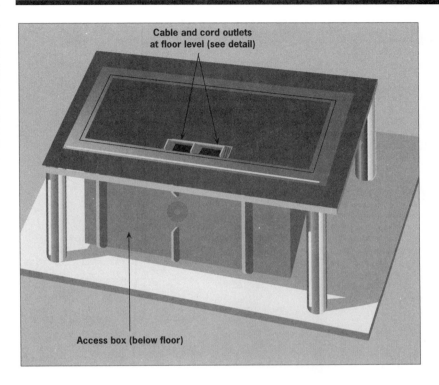

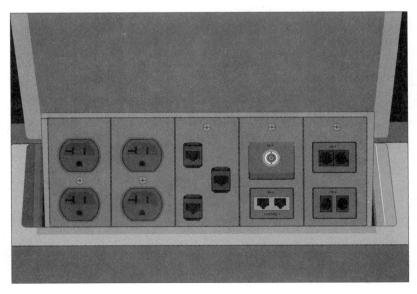

Figure 3.12

This AMPIX printed-circuit-board assembly and other similar modules are installed in a mounting track to build a distribution and cross-connect system. The use of printed-circuit-board connections gives extremely low levels of crosstalk and high reliability.

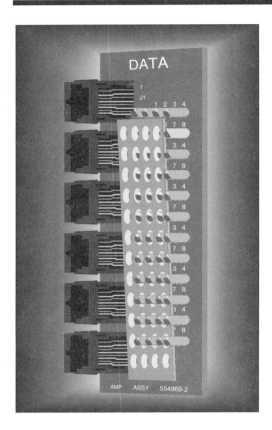

Mod-Tap Products

Mod-Tap's product line stresses flexibility. The company markets products that meet the requirements of AT&T, IBM, Digital, and many other companies as well as standards committees. Mod-Tap also has an excellent line of fiber-optic products that range from the cable itself to connectors and splicing equipment and supplies. The company is a single source of supply for a wide variety of products that range from wall plates and connectors to all the components of a distribution frame. Unlike AT&T, Mod-Tap products support a wide range of wiring specifications, including those of AT&T, Digital, IBM, and Wang.

The Mod-Tap Universal System Outlet (USO), shown in Figure 3.13, provides an attractive and flexible way to terminate horizontal wiring at a node. You can snap various modules into the mounting box to customize the connections appearing at any wall plate or panel. This flexibility reduces the size and cost of installations while still making it easy to respond to moves and changes.

Figure 3.13

The Mod-Tap Universal System Outlet allows you to snap various connection modules into wall plates, surface mounting-modules, and equipment racks. You can select from among RJ-45, BNC, fiber, video, and many other connectors.

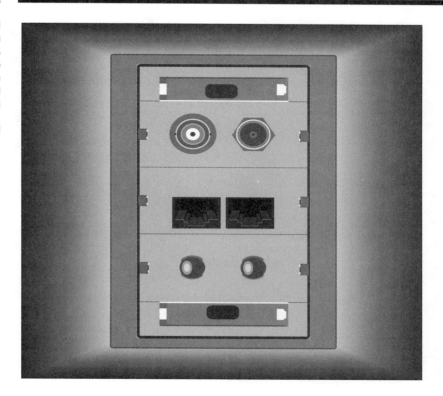

Anixter's Cable Model

Anixter is a worldwide distributor of wiring-system products. It is also a service and technology company with a technical support staff of specialists and engineers who can help customers choose products and answer questions relating to design, industry specifications, and installation. The company's place in history as the developer of the multilevel model of performance for cables is assured. Anixter's model includes five levels that describe the performance and electrical characteristics of wiring, ranging from the most common telephone wire used in residences to sophisticated twisted-pair wire capable of moving data at 100 megabits per second.

The Anixter cable-level designations led a major evolution in the industry. The UL and EIA/TIA both use an evolved version of the Anixter cable model, and we'll describe the total model with all additions later in this chapter.

Amid the popularity of unshielded twisted-pair wiring, it is worth repeating that most of the wire installed for telephone systems does not meet the standards for LAN data transmission over 1 megabit per second. The telephone wiring in residences and many small businesses is typically a cable carrying four untwisted wires called "quad." Quad is fine for simple telephone installations and for very low-speed data applications, but that's all.

Similarly, some PBX telephone systems use a twisted-pair wire. Even though it is twisted, this wire doesn't have the correct electrical properties to match the requirements of modern high-speed local-area network adapters. The Anixter Level 1 and Level 2 specifications describe these products with lower levels of performance.

■ National Electrical Code (NEC)

The National Electrical Code (NEC) is established by the National Fire Protection Association (NFPA). The language of the code is designed so that it can be adopted as law through legislative procedure. You'll see the term NEC used widely in cable catalogs, and you shouldn't confuse it with specifications from a major international equipment manufacturer with the same initials.

In general terms, the NEC describes how a cable burns. During a building fire, a cable going between walls, up an elevator shaft, or through an air-handling plenum could become a torch that carries the flame from one floor or one part of the building to another. Since the coverings of cables and wires are typically plastic, they can create noxious smoke when they burn. Several organizations, including UL, have established standards for flame and smoke that apply to LAN cables. However, the NEC contains the standards most widely supported by local licensing and inspection officials. The standards, among other things, set a limit to the maximum amount of time the cable burns after a flame is applied. Other standards, developed by the NFPA and adopted by the American National Standards Institute (ANSI), also describe the type and amount of smoke a burning cable can generate.

While the industry recognizes and generally conforms to the NEC standards, every individual municipality can decide whether or not to adopt the latest version of the NEC for local use. In other words, the NEC standards might or might not be a part of your local fire or building codes. In either case, we urge you to select, for your application, cable that meets the NEC standards.

Type Codes

You'll see NEC type codes listed in catalogs of cables and supplies. These codes classify specific categories of products for specific uses, as shown here:

Type of Cable	Description
OFC (fiber-optic)	Contains metal conductors, inserted for strength
OFN (fiber-optic)	Contains no metal
CMP (communications plenum)	Passed tests showing a limited spread of flame and low production of smoke. Plenum cable is typically coated with a special jacket material such as Teflon. The letter P in this code defines a plenum as a channel or ductwork fabricated for handling air. A false ceiling or floor is not a plenum.
CMR (communications riser)	The letter R shows that the cable has passed similar but slightly different tests for the spread of flame and production of smoke. For example, riser cable is tested for its burning properties in a vertical position. According to the code, you must use cable rated for riser service whenever a cable penetrates a floor and a ceiling. Riser cables typically have a polyvinyl chloride (PVC) outer jacket.

Generally, you'll find LAN cables listed in the category of type CM for communications or type MP for multipurpose. Some companies choose to run their cables through testing as remote-control or power-limited circuit cables CL2 or CL3 (class 2 or class 3) general tests instead of through the CM or CP tests, but the flame and smoke criteria are generally the same for all tests. The differences between these markings concern the amount of electrical power that could run through the cable under the worst case. MP cable is subjected to tests that assume the most power-handling capability, with CM, CL3, and CL2 going through tests with decreasing levels of power handling.

■ The EIA/TIA-568 (SP-2840) Standard

The Electronic Industries Association/Telecommunications Industry Association (EIA/TIA) is a U.S. standards body with a long history of issuing standards for communications systems including, for example, EIA232 for serial communications ports. The EIA/TIA tackled the problem of specifying LAN cables by starting with the Anixter Level 5 model, but the EIA/TIA calls the divisions "categories" instead of levels. Amp and other companies worked in the EIA/TIA to expand the model to account for other categories of products, including coaxial cable and fiber-optic cable. The result is the EIA/TIA-568 Standard for Commercial Building Telecommunications Wiring. Note: The EIA/TIA standard is being renamed to SP-2840. However, the old name will probably remain in use for some time.

The primary advantage of EIA/TIA-568 is its publication as an open standard without the stamp of any single vendor. You can select and specify cable that meets a specific category of the EIA/TIA-568 standard and expect to get comparable bids back from a variety of vendors. Note, however, that the EIA/TIA categories are not tied to the NEC specifications, and they don't deal with shielded twisted-pair wiring. (As we'll describe later in this chapter, UL finally ties performance to safety.)

The EIA/TIA-568 standard describes both the performance specifications of the cable and its installation. However, the standard still leaves the network-system designer room for options and expansion. The standard calls for running two cables, one for voice and one for data, to each outlet. One of the two cables must be 4-pair unshielded twisted pair for voice. You can choose to run the data on another unshielded twisted-pair cable or on coax. If you elect to run fiber to the desktop, it can't displace the copper data cable.

Here is an overview of the cable-performance specification described in EIA/TIA-568:

- Category 1: Overall, EIA/TIA-568 says very little about the technical specifications in Category 1 or Category 2. The descriptions that follow are for general information. Category 1 cable is typically 22 AWG or 24 AWG untwisted wire, with a wide range of impedance and attenuation values. Category 1 is not recommended for data in general and certainly not for signaling speeds over 1 megabit per second.

- Category 2: This category of cable is the same as the Anixter Level 2 cable specification, and it is derived from the IBM Type 3 cable specification. This cable uses 22 or 24 AWG solid wire in twisted pairs. It is tested to a maximum bandwidth of 1 MHz and is not tested for near-end crosstalk. You can use this cable for IBM 3270 and AS/400 computer connections and for Apple LocalTalk.

- Category 3: This category of cable is the same as the Anixter Level 3, and generally is the minimum level of cable quality you should allow in new installations. Category 3 uses 24 AWG solid wire in twisted pairs. This wire displays a typical impedance of 100 ohms, and is tested for attenuation and near-end crosstalk through 16 MHz. Useful for data transmission at speeds up to 16 megabits per second, this wire is the lowest standard you should use for 10Base-T installations, and it is sufficient for 4 megabit-per-second Token-Ring.

- Category 4: The same as the Anixter Level 4 cable, Category 4 cable can have 22 AWG or 24 AWG solid wire in twisted pairs. This cable has a typical impedance of 100 ohms, and is tested for performance at a bandwidth of 20 MHz. Category 4 cable is formally rated for a maximum signaling speed of 20 MHz, so it is good cable to install if you think you'll run 16 megabit-per-second Token-Ring over unshielded twisted-pair wire. Category 4 cable also works well for 10Base-T installations.

- Category 5: This is the performance specification we recommend for all new installations. This is 22 or 24 AWG unshielded twisted-pair cable with a 100 ohm impedance. Tested at a bandwidth of 100 MHz, it can handle data signaling at 100 megabits per second under specified conditions. Category 5 cable is a high-quality medium with growing applications for transmitting video, images, and very high-speed data.

Trying to describe the EIA/TIA-568 standard and the category system in a book is like trying to paint a moving train. The standard evolves through an interactive committee process, and change, particularly expansion, is constant. For example, because IBM's 150-ohm, shielded Type 1 and Type 9 cable is so important in the market, we expect to see it accommodated in the standard. There are proposals to integrate Thinnet Ethernet coaxial cable, 62.5/125 micron multimode fiber, and single-mode-fiber cable (used for long distance connections) into the specification.

■ Underwriters Laboratories (UL)

Local fire- and building-code regulators try to use standards like those of the NEC, but insurance groups and other regulators often specify the standards of the Underwriters Laboratories. UL has safety standards for cables similar to those of the NEC. UL 444 is the Standard for Safety for Communications Cable. UL 13 is the Standard for Safety for Power-Limited Circuit Cable. Network cable might fall into either category. UL tests and evaluates samples of cable and then, after granting a UL listing, the organization conducts follow-up tests and inspections. This independent testing and follow-through make the UL markings valuable symbols to buyers.

In an interesting and unique action, the people at UL stirred safety and performance together in a program designed to make selecting or specifying a cable easier. UL's LAN Certification Program addresses not only safety, but performance. IBM authorized UL to verify 150-ohm STP to IBM performance specifications, and UL established a data-transmission, performance-level marking program that covers 100-ohm twisted-pair cable. UL adopted the EIA/TIA-568 performance standard and, through that, some aspects of the Anixter cable performance model. There is a small inconsistency: The UL program deals with both shielded and unshielded twisted-pair wire, while the EIA/TIA-568 standard focuses on unshielded wire.

The UL markings range from Level I through Level V. You can tell a UL level from an Anixter level because the UL uses Roman numerals. As we described, IBM's cable specifications range from Type 1 through Type 9, while the EIA/TIA has Category 1 through Category 5. It's easy to become confused by the similarly numbered levels and types. The UL level markings deal with performance and safety, so the products that merit UL level markings also meet the appropriate NEC MP, CM, or CL specifications as well as the EIA/TIA standard for a specific category.

Companies whose cables earn these UL markings display them on the outer jacket as, for example, Level I, LVL I, or LEV I. Here is a summary of the UL level markings:

- The UL Level I marking meets appropriate NEC and UL 444 safety requirements. No specific performance specifications.

- The UL Level II marking meets the performance requirements of EIA/TIA-568 Category 2 and IBM Cable Plan Type 3 cable. Meets appropriate NEC and UL 444 safety requirements. Acceptable for 4-megabit Token-Ring, but not for higher-speed data applications such as 10Base-T.

- The UL Level III marking meets the performance requirements of EIA/TIA-568 Category 3 and NEC and UL 444 safety requirements. Lowest acceptable marking for LAN applications.

- The UL Level IV marking meets the performance requirements of EIA/TIA-568 Category 4 and NEC and UL 444 safety requirements.

- The UL Level V marking meets the performance requirements of EIA/TIA-568 Category 5 and NEC and UL 444 safety requirements. The right choice for new LAN installations.

■ Evolution

The standards committees will continue meeting. They constantly make proposals and usually issue major updates every five years. New technologies, plus the desire of companies to find a tiny marketing edge for new products, will press for evolutionary changes to the standards for network wiring and cabling. Also, other standards bodies will follow the path of Anixter, EIA/TIA, and UL. For example, Standards Committee 25 of the International

Standards Organization (ISO)/International Electrotechnical Commission (IEC) Joint Technical Committee 1 has developed a framework of international standards (probably known as ISO/IEC JTC1/SC25 with further numbers and letters). This framework applies to Token-Ring cabling and a generic structured cabling system. Fortunately, the emerging ISO/IEC standards closely follow the EIA/TIA standards, but there will be some differences.

Your cable plant must last a long time. Following the EIA/TIA and ISO/IEC standards will ensure payback on your investment and successful operation of networks that are critical to your business.

- *Ethernet*
- *Token-Ring*
- *ARCnet*
- *Newer Standards*

4

LAN Combinations

Willy knew there would be a problem, because these folks weren't speaking the same language. On his truck's two-way radio, he'd heard the New Guy ask Bill Owens, one of the more experienced installers, if he had a "mau" in his truck. The New Guy was troubleshooting at an old and valued client, and apparently he thought he could quickly solve the problem by replacing the MAU. But Willy knew that these two guys were using the same term for different items.

As Willy pulled into the parking lot, the New Guy was wearing a puzzled expression as he tore apart a cardboard box nearly two feet wide and a few inches high.

"I asked Bill for a MAU, and this is what he gave me," the New Guy explained to Willy. "Unless there's a dozen of them in here, this isn't the right thing."

"You went to Hewlett-Packard system schools, right?" Willy asked. When the New Guy nodded, Willy explained, "HP calls an external transceiver for 10Base-T wiring a media attachment unit or MAU, and that's what you wanted—a transceiver to attach to the AUI port on an Ethernet adapter, so it can make a 10Base-T connection. Well, Bill went to IBM school. At IBM a MAU is a multistation access unit—a wiring hub. What you have there is a wiring hub for token-ring."

"Oh," the New Guy replied, "no wonder he asked me if I wanted a MAU for unshielded twisted-pair. I thought he was being funny."

Willy tossed the New Guy a package about the size of a deck of playing cards. "Here, use this external 10Base-T transceiver and also remember to use plain old English whenever possible. Even when folks are familiar with the standards, it's still better to describe what you want as simply as possible. After all, standards are wonderful things—that's why we have so many of them!"

The ARCnet, Ethernet, and Token-Ring specifications were each developed in a vacuum. The designers of ARCnet were unaware of the efforts of the Ethernet designers, even though the developments occurred nearly simultaneously. IBM also designed Token-Ring from a clean slate. In all cases, specifications for using unshielded twisted-pair wire were overlayed onto the existing architecture—primarily in response to customer demand.

In this chapter, we provide an easy guide to the generally accepted specifications for cabling ARCnet, Ethernet, and token-ring systems. This guide is intended as an initial planning tool; you might find that the distances and configuration you hope to implement are difficult to execute under a specific architecture. It should also be useful as a reference when you want to expand the network. Limitations on factors such as overall cable length can make it very expensive to add just one more node to the network in the future.

The factors we provide are for planning purposes only. Although some companies offer wiring hubs and network interface cards capable of spanning greater distances than the ones we present, some electrical environments will dictate much shorter limits. In Chapter 9, we discuss testing and certification. After using this chapter to plan a cable installation, it is wise to test and get a profile of it. If you are using 16 megabit or faster signaling, certification of the installation is especially important to your network's success and perhaps to your future employment as well.

Now let's look at the generally accepted copper cabling plans for the three major networking architectures. We'll talk about fiber optic cabling in Chapter 8.

■ Ethernet

The three primary types of Ethernet connections are thin coaxial cable, thick coaxial cable, and unshielded twisted-pair wire. Separate rules apply to each type of cabling, but before we look at each situation, let's review some overall vocabulary.

Ethernet cabling is primarily based on the concept of a *trunk cable*. A *trunk segment* is a piece of cable with a terminator at each end. Inside each terminator, an electrical component called a *resistor* soaks up signals reaching the end of the cable so they don't reflect back up the cable and create patterns of conflicting signals.

Individual trunk segments are linked by devices called *repeaters*. A repeater regenerates the electrical signals to restore the strength they lost through cable attenuation, but the carrier-sense multiple access cable-sharing scheme limits the number of repeaters allowed in a network cable system.

Generally, you can have four repeaters in an Ethernet system linking five trunk segments, but only three of those trunk segments can have nodes attached. Two of the trunks are, in Ethernet terms, *unpopulated*, but serve to extend the network between populated segments.

The IEEE 802.3 committee designates each style of architecture according to signaling speed, type of signaling, and the maximum cable length (in meters) of one trunk segment. Here's an example of how the IEEE 802.3 designation system works: The thick coaxial cable uses a 10 megabit-per-second signaling speed and baseband signaling (described in Chapter 1), and the standard allows a maximum of 500 meters of cable on one trunk segment. A system that conforms to these standards is designated as 10Base5.

Thin coaxial cabling, also known informally as Cheapernet or thin Ethernet, has poorer electrical characteristics, so the IEEE standard limits thin Ethernet systems to a trunk segment length of 185 meters, which is close enough to 200 meters for this type of cabling system to be designated as 10Base2. Ethernet over UTP is a special case that is referred to as *10Base-T* (twisted). The term 10Base-F describes fiber-optic cable connections. A draft standard for signaling at 100 megabits over some yet-to-be determined distance is known as 100Base-X.

However, the IEEE designation doesn't specify the physical arrangement of the cables, or what is called the *physical topology*, shown in Figure 4.1. The 10Base2 and 10Base5 systems use a linear bus configuration, which means that the nodes connect to the cable and it proceeds in a linear fashion between the nodes. This arrangement is the most economical in terms of the number of feet of cable it uses, but one break in the cable or a bad connection at any point will disable the entire network. The 10Base-T system uses a star wiring arrangement that is more reliable but also more expensive due to the costs of additional cable and hardware. Also, 10Base-T does not rely on external terminators. Wiring hubs can contain connectors for each Ethernet wiring scheme, allowing combinations of the topologies to meet special needs.

Thick Ethernet

A 10Base5 thick Ethernet system uses a trunk or backbone cable with a 50 ohm terminator at each end. The "frozen yellow garden hose" thick Ethernet cable (named for its appearance and handling characteristics) typically runs through a false ceiling or floor. When you want to connect to a node, you use a device called a *vampire tap* that pierces the outer shield with a metal fang and makes contact with the center conductor. This seemingly radical surgery results in surprisingly reliable connections. Another type of tap that uses connectors is available, but in our experience, the connectors make this type of tap less reliable in the long run than the vampire tap.

The thick Ethernet cable tap contains electronic components that sense the electrical carrier on the cable, so generally it is referred to as a *transceiver*. A piece of multiconductor shielded cable, called the *transceiver cable*, connects the tap to the network adapter. The transceiver cable connects to the networking interface card's *attachment unit interface* (AUI) socket. The connector used on the AUI socket, and the transceiver cable is called a *DIX connector*.

The maximum length of a single trunk segment is 1,640 feet (500 meters), and the maximum overall cable length connected by repeaters is 8,200 feet (2,500 meters). The standard allows 100 nodes on each trunk segment, and the minimum distance between transceivers is 8 feet (2.5 meters). The maximum length of transceiver cable is 165 feet (50 meters), but transceiver cable is expensive, so you'll probably want to keep the cable runs short. Plan for the backbone cable run to use unspliced lengths of thick Ethernet cable between the nodes whenever possible.

Figure 4.1

Here are the three standard Ethernet topologies. The thick and thin Ethernet systems use two slightly different types of coaxial trunk cables with terminators at each end.

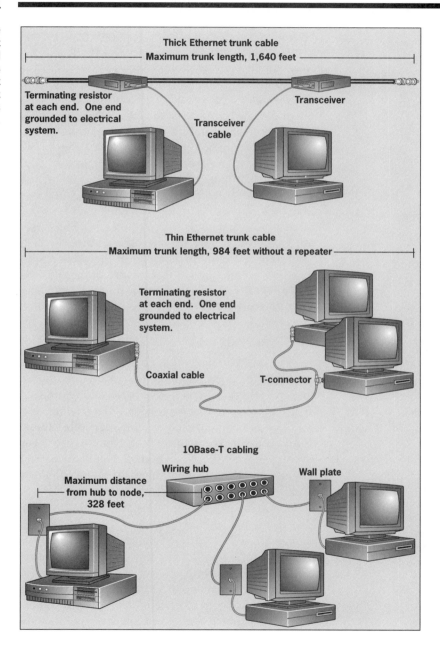

Thick Ethernet trunk cable
Maximum trunk length, 1,640 feet

Terminating resistor at each end. One end grounded to electrical system.

Transceiver

Transceiver cable

Thin Ethernet trunk cable
Maximum trunk length, 984 feet without a repeater

Terminating resistor at each end. One end grounded to electrical system.

Coaxial cable

T-connector

10Base-T cabling

Wiring hub

Wall plate

Maximum distance from hub to node, 328 feet

The outside of the jacket of the thick Ethernet backbone cable has distance markers on it that show the quarter wavelength points. It's important that the terminators are installed precisely on a marker at each end. If they are and you tap into the cable at those points marked in between, the transceiver detects the correct impedance. If you miss the point by more than a few inches, then theoretically the impedance mismatch could set up reflections within the cable that would lead to lost packets. According to the specification, one of the terminators must be attached to the building electrical ground. This ground wire usually connects to a mounting screw on a wall socket.

In practice, people report that thick Ethernet works despite all types of mishandling. If you ever suspect you might have a problem with the thick Ethernet backbone cable, look instead for a bad network interface card or a transceiver with the Signal Quality Error (SQE) switch turned on. SQE is an old feature that causes more problems than it solves. Just remember the mnemonic used by installers (namely, that SQE has three letters, like the word "off") and you'll know what to do with the switch. Thick Ethernet is difficult to install because of the diameter of the cable and the complex hardware required for every connection. Because of these factors and the growing popularity of UTP, you won't see many new thick Ethernet installations, but once it is in the walls, it should work until the building falls down.

Thin Ethernet

If you're sure you'll never need a network cable system with an overall length greater than 3,000 feet, then installing thin Ethernet makes more sense than thick Ethernet. As Figure 4.2 illustrates, thin coaxial cable Ethernet systems can not use any type of "drop" cable—an extension between the backbone cable and the node. The backbone cable travels from node to node without drops or transceiver cables, and uses a T-connector to make the connection at each node. Each end of each trunk cable has a terminating resistor, and one of the terminating resistors on each trunk cable should be grounded to the building's electrical system.

Generally, a thin Ethernet system includes a maximum of five trunk cable segments linked by repeaters. Each trunk segment can have a maximum length of 607 feet (185 meters), so the total system can have an overall length of 3,035 feet (925 meters). If you don't use repeaters, you may have one trunk segment with an overall maximum length of 984 feet (300 meters). Each trunk cable can have a maximum of 30 nodes, and the minimum distance between nodes is 1.5 feet (0.45 meters). While 30 nodes is the standard, many models of LAN adapters are designed to allow up to 100 nodes on a trunk cable.

Figure 4.2

Never use a drop cable in
a thin Ethernet wiring plan.
The trunk cable must go
from node to node.

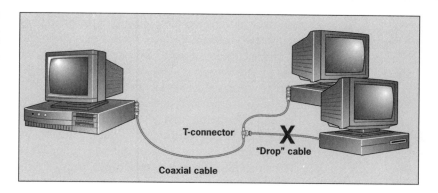

10Base-T

What is at the root of the popularity of 10Base-T, the standard for Ethernet
signaling over unshielded twisted-pair wire? Well, the answer is *not* because
it allows you to use the telephone wiring in your walls! Unless you have a
premise distribution system installed by AT&T, Northern Telecom, or another major vendor, you will almost always have to rewire for any network
installation, except perhaps ARCnet. Even if you do have a high-grade telephone PBX cabling system in your walls, chances are good that after an extensive survey, you'll have to add cables, replace wall plates, and take other
upgrade actions to prepare for network installation, so don't be mislead by
false promises of no cost for 10Base-T cabling.

UTP is popular because it's cheaper and thinner than the other alternatives. Also, people feel comfortable with the technology. But it's quite likely
that you'll have to pull new cable to run 10Base-T. If you do opt for this installation, we strongly recommend going all the way and using the highest
available grade of UTP in a certified installation—particularly if your employment depends on the reliable operation of the network!

The 10Base-T plan specifies a wiring hub, cable arranged in a star configuration, and unshielded twisted-pair cable. Each node has a separate cable
run, not to exceed 328 feet (100 meters) from the node to the hub. There are
no terminators. Some vendors market adapters and hubs that can extend this
distance, but it's wise to use greater distance as a bonus and not to plan on it
as a necessity. You can mix the other types of Ethernet wiring schemes and
10Base-T in the same network, because hubs often have AUI connectors for
thin Ethernet, thick Ethernet, or even fiber-optic cable transceivers.

The star wiring configuration prevents a single bad connector or piece
of cable from bringing down the entire network as it can with thin Ethernet.
Modern 10Base-T hubs and adapters offer a built-in link-integrity test feature

that causes a light-emitting diode to glow when the node's network interface card has power and the electrical connection is good. This lets you determine at a glance whether you have a cabling problem. The hub can recognize certain trouble conditions and isolate or "partition" the offending segment so it doesn't impact the rest of the network. Of course, if the bad cable segment leads to your only server, you still will lose network services, but the cause of the outage should be obvious and easy to repair. High reliability and easy maintenance are prime features of 10Base-T.

Wiring hubs come in all shapes and sizes. Some hubs are built onto adapter cards that fit inside a PC. Others, like the D-Link hub shown in Figure 4.3, are small cabinets about the size of a hardback book that some people stick onto the side of a desk. Both of these solutions are only appropriate for small networks of less than 6 to 12 nodes. Expect to pay about $25 to $30 per port for these products. The 10Base-T standard allows up to 1,000 nodes per cable segment, which is more than you're ever likely to use. You'll separate your LAN into more cable segments long before you get to 100 plus nodes.

Figure 4.3

This small D-Link wiring hub for 10Base-T offers economy and good service, but these types of hubs have limited expansion capabilities.

NOTE. *The 10Base-T three-repeater rule limits the number of hubs in a daisy-chain to three.*

However, the 10Base-T wiring scheme contains a subtle trap. Many network planners start small, with a standalone hub that can accommodate 8 to 12 nodes. When the network grows, they buy another hub and connect the two hubs in a daisy-chain. This growth pattern continues through the third hub, but if they try adding a fourth hub in this manner, they start getting collisions, runt (short) packets, and overruns (long packets). The 10Base-T three-repeater rule essentially says that you can only use three repeaters between major LAN segments. If you add a fourth repeater, the timing of the packets can be impaired and the CSMA/CD media-sharing scheme breaks down. Some companies have marketed hubs with tight timing so that you can have four repeaters, but the basic rule is a limit of three hubs.

You avoid conflicts with the three-repeater rule and gain the ability to easily expand your network by using a *chassis hub*. A chassis hub that takes add-in module strips, each of which is full of port connectors. The chassis interconnects the strips across a very fast data bus, so adding more nodes doesn't upset the CSMA/CD timing.

Many people have been painfully caught unaware by the three-repeater rule. Small wiring hubs with a fixed number of ports are initially inexpensive, compared to hubs with a chassis and a data bus backplane, which initially seem very costly. But this is a classic case of "pay now or pay later." If you don't pay for the expansion capability in the beginning, you might have to throw away your investment and start from scratch later.

However, there is a middle ground for conservative LAN planners. 3Com pioneered a line of what are called "stackable" 10Base-T wiring hubs, and other companies like Asanté have marketed competing products. These fixed hubs have an external connection that acts like a backplane. You can connect short special cable links between these hubs, and each stack appears as a single repeater. So, by investing a few more dollars per port in the beginning for stackable hubs, your installation can smoothly expand into a manageable system of wiring hubs.

■ Token-Ring

The IEEE 802.5 token-ring system also uses a wiring hub as the center of the cable plan. The token-ring architecture was originally designed to operate with shielded twisted-pair cable, but LAN managers and designers quickly demanded UTP connections. IBM delivered a device that the company calls a "media filter," which mates the STP connector on its network interface cards to UTP. Now IBM and many other companies market interface cards and wiring hubs designed for UTP.

If you only have 4 megabit-per-second token-ring, you can run it over Category 3 UTP. You'll see published specifications for running 16 megabit token-ring over Category 3 cable, but we don't recommend it. We think 16 megabit-per-second token-ring requires an EIA/TIA 568 Category 5 UTP installation.

The number of active network nodes is a more important factor in token-ring than in any other networking scheme. Each time a token-ring node activates its network interface card, a voltage is imposed on a relay in the wiring hub. The relay in the hub pulls in and inserts the node's cable segment into the active ring, effectively changing the size of the overall network. In other networking schemes, the overall length of the cable stays the same when stations enter or leave the network, but as Figure 4.4 illustrates, activating a token-ring node automatically increases the overall active network cable length.

Figure 4.4

A token-ring network is a complex arrangement of nodes, cables, and wiring hubs with active components. When a node activates its network interface card, it applies a voltage across the cable to a relay in the wiring hub. The relay activates, breaks the existing ring of cable, and inserts the added cable out to the new node. Every time a node activates, it increases the overall length of the network cable.

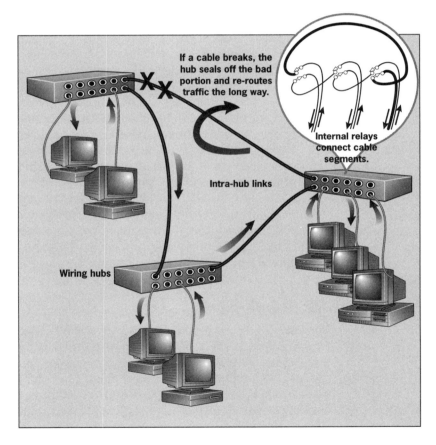

In this token-ring scheme, the maximum length of all STP cable is 1,312 feet at 4 megabits per second, and 590 feet at 16 megabits per second. In a system that uses UTP cable, the maximum length of the total cable is 738 feet at 4 megabits per second, and 328 feet at 16 megabits per second.

MTD = ECL + (lobe length * nodes) + loopback

There is a complex interaction between the cable length, the number of wiring hubs, the links between the wiring hubs, and the number of overall active nodes on a token-ring network. The picture is made even fuzzier by some vendors who have introduced devices called "powered" wiring hubs that they claim provide reliable operation at six times the distance of standard hubs. On the bottom line, it's difficult to give you hard-and-fast guidelines for maximum cable length, because the manufacturer's specifications vary so widely. We suggest you consult with the vendors of token-ring equipment before finalizing your token-ring cabling plan.

Token-ring relies on the concept of *maximum total cable distance* (MTD), which is used to describe the maximum amount of cable in the ring that you may use without employing powered, or *active*, hubs that regenerate the signals. The typical MTD for equipment using shielded twisted-pair wire is 1,312 feet (400 meters) at 4 megabits, and 590 feet (180 meters) at 16 megabits. The MTD for Category 5 UTP is 738 feet (225 meters) at 4 megabits and 328 feet (100 meters) at 16 megabits.

The MTD includes all of the actual physical cable and a factor called *equivalent cable length* (ECL) that represents the signal loss inside the wiring hub. Each manufacturer provides an ECL for the specific make and model of hub, but an average figure is 8 feet (2.5 meters) for STP hubs and 30 feet (8.5 meters) for UTP. You only add the ECL factor into the MTD equation one time for each hub, that is, you don't add an ECL for every active port.

The computation becomes very complex if you consider every contingency involving multiple hubs. Token-ring has a self-healing feature that makes it possible for a hub to automatically loop-back and create its own ring if a connection between hubs breaks. This loop-back could theoretically almost double the active cable length as a hub sends frames back the long way around the ring. Planning for the worst case is prudent, but it requires careful study of a cable diagram, and it will limit you to using very conservative cable lengths.

Here are some practical token-ring planning guidelines for shielded and unshielded twisted-pair cable. These guidelines are for 4 megabit-per-second token-ring systems. Generally, you'll have to cut the maximum distance between the node and hub in half for 16 megabit-per-second token-ring. However, the specifications for some manufacturer's equipment will give you much greater distances.

- If you run 4 megabit token-ring on shielded twisted-pair wire, you can use as much as 150 feet (45 meters) of cable between each node and the wiring hub. Two wiring hubs can be separated by the same 150 foot distance, but the maximum overall length between wiring hubs can't exceed

400 feet (120 meters). An 8-foot adapter cable is allowed between the wall jack and the node. Theoretically, you can have as many as 260 nodes on the ring using shielded twisted-pair cable, but you'll probably exceed the MTD before you exceed the node limit.

- On Category 5 unshielded twisted-pair, you are limited to a maximum of 132 nodes on the main ring. Limiting the number of nodes automatically limits the maximum amount of cable on the overall ring. However, the IEEE 802.5 standard for token-ring over UTP contains very complex guidelines that require on-site measurement of signals between wire pairs, attenuation, and even temperature. In short, you will need a qualified and well-equipped installation team.

- The shielded twisted-pair wire suggested for token-ring networks offers high-quality networking, but it also carries a steep price tag. In installations that won't suffer from a lot of electrical noise, UTP makes sense.

■ ARCnet

ARCnet evolved backwards. The original ARCnet plan, developed in the late 1960s, called for using wiring hubs with a dedicated run of coaxial cable between each node and the hub, which is now a key feature of the much newer Ethernet 10Base-T and token-ring networks. But in the 1980s, various companies delivered ARCnet adapters that could use both coaxial and unshielded twisted-pair wire in a station-to-station configuration like the linear bus configuration of the original thin Ethernet.

ARCnet is a bad news/good news networking system. Its slow signaling speed of 2.5 megabits per second won't support a large number of high-powered PCs trying to run busy applications, but the slow signaling speed does facilitate using long cable runs and lower quality UTP cable. Unlike 10Base-T or token-ring, you can use ARCnet on voice grade telephone PBX cable that might already be in the walls of your building. An EIA/TIA Category 2 cable installation will work fine with ARCnet.

In its standard configuration (see Figure 4.5), ARCnet uses RG-62 coaxial cable, which is the same cable IBM used in its 3270 mainframe terminal system. You can have as much as 2,000 feet of coax between a node and its powered hub. Powered hubs in ARCnet systems are not expensive, as they are in token-ring networks, so they are commonly used. ARCnet allows for even lower-cost unpowered hubs, but the maximum cable run between a node and an unpowered hub is 100 feet. Because ARCnet doesn't depend on the CSMA/CD listen-before-talk techniques to regulate how the cable is shared, timing is not critical and, as Figure 4.5 illustrates, the maximum node-to-node distances can be as much as 20,000 feet. Under UTP, you can use as much as 400 feet of voice-grade cable between the node and wiring hub.

Figure 4.5

The classical ARCnet system uses wiring hubs with coaxial cable in a star physical topology. A few manufacturers sell interface cards that use UTP in a bus configuration.

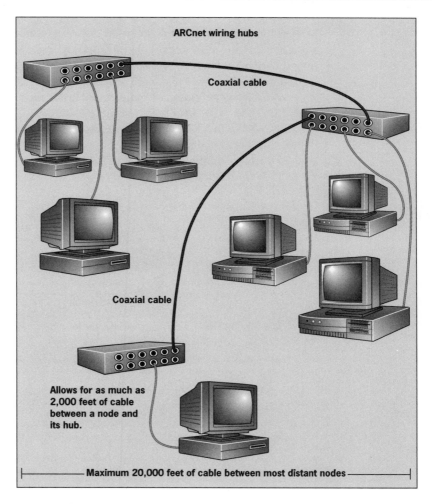

ARCnet wiring hubs

Coaxial cable

Coaxial cable

Allows for as much as 2,000 feet of cable between a node and its hub.

Maximum 20,000 feet of cable between most distant nodes

Some specific brands and models of ARCnet adapters allow you to use either coax or UTP in a daisy-chain or linear bus configuration. The overall length of the single coaxial cable span in linear bus is 1,000 feet, and the maximum overall length of UTP is 400 feet. However, because of the difficulty in matching overall impedance and signal levels, you can only have ten nodes on the cable. Some companies suggest that you can connect a string of daisy-chained nodes to a wiring hub; however, we don't recommend it, because we have found that these types of installations are often unreliable.

■ Newer Standards

Technology doesn't stand still, and many organizations have expressed needs for a networking system capable of signaling faster than the Ethernet 10 megabits per second or the token-ring 16 megabits per second. Systems with signaling speeds of 100 and even 155 megabits per second are evolving, but these systems won't carry the requirements for the specialized cabling systems that came with Ethernet, token-ring, and ARCnet. Instead, they will use either EIA/TIA Category 5 cabling, a combination of several Category 3 cables, or fiber-optic cable. In any case, a good Category 5 installation is a wise investment in the future.

- *1Wiring Hub Management*
- *Cabinet and Chassis Hubs*
- *Differentiation through Management*
- *Network Management Architectures*
- *Network Management and Troubleshooting*

5

Managing through the Hub

As the kicker's toe touched the ball to start the third quarter, Willy's beeper started to vibrate on his belt. After the runback, he read the message on the LCD screen asking him to call the network manager at one of OK Cable's clients, a local hospital. He considered using a pay phone, but then he walked down the stadium's spiral ramp to the parking lot gate and negotiated a pass to get back in.

His cable service truck usually wasn't his idea of Sunday afternoon transportation, but it was his turn to be on emergency call, and driving the truck to the game was a good compromise to staying at home. He disarmed the truck's alarms, sat inside, and savored being out of the wind while the cellular phone woke up and negotiated with a local cell site. Then he called Janet Jackson at the hospital.

"Willy!" she exclaimed. "Thanks for calling so quickly. I can't get ahold of anybody else, and our network is down. The doctors can't enter patient records, the emergency room can't do billing, and I'm in hot water! I've checked everything on the server and clients. I think it's gotta be cable."

Willy winced. He was proud of the hospital's cabling system—he had designed it and supervised its installation. A fiber-optic backbone fed a series of wiring hubs that provided excellent physical isolation. "What about the hub management system? What's it showing?" he asked.

"I can't get into it either. The management console can't talk to the hubs across the network to get any updated data."

"Janet, I'm going to call into the hub management system through the RS-232 modem connection. I'll call you back in a few minutes." Willy knew that Janet's management console didn't have a modem she could use to dial into the hub's serial port as a backdoor connection. It wasn't the cost of the modem that drove this decision, but rather the monthly recurring cost of the usually unused telephone line. Willy reflected that some forms of insurance seem awfully expensive until you need them.

He booted his laptop computer and connected an RS-232 cable from the laptop's serial port to a battery-operated modem about the size of a deck of playing cards. Then he made a connection from the modem to a jack in the side of his truck's cellular phone. The resulting chain of cables and devices offended his sense of neatness, but he knew from experience that it worked.

The telephone number for the hospital's hub management system was in Willy's communications software. OK Cable paid for the phone line under the hospital's monthly maintenance plan. Actually, the hospital paid for the line through OK Cable, but it seemed to get through the budget that way.

Willy dialed the telephone number on the cellular handset, and when he heard the modem answer, he entered the command ATX0D on the laptop's keyboard to bring the modem on line. The two modems negotiated a 9,600-bit-per-second connection, the software's script sent the appropriate password, and he was in. The script had previously set up a long dropout time in the modem so that changes in the phone's cellular connection, which can take place even if you're standing still, didn't cause the modem to lose the carrier.

Willy's terminal emulation software didn't have the pretty windows or moving chart displays of the management console, but the network's problem was immediately apparent when he looked at the network traffic display. One adapter in the network was jabbering—it was constantly transmitting packets without listening. This caused what appeared to be a constant series of collisions and all of the other, well-behaved adapters were simply waiting for a clear channel. This hardware malfunction didn't have anything to do with Willy's cable, but he could fix it.

He entered the command mode in the wiring hub software and gave the command to partition or isolate the offending node. This caused the hub to literally disconnect that port from the rest of the network. Then he went back to the traffic monitor screen and saw the server start to announce its presence on the network. He was disconnecting the modem cables when his cellular phone rang.

"Everything is up!" Janet exclaimed. "You're magic."

"Magic is simply knowledge you don't have yet," Willy observed. "Go to the wiring hubs and see which port has a partition light lit. Then change out the network interface card in the node connected to that port and reset the port."

Willy entered the call in his service log—emergency calls on Sunday afternoon weren't in the hospital's maintenance contract—locked the truck, and headed back to the stadium. With luck, he'd see the whole fourth quarter.

■ Wiring Hub Management

Wiring hubs are a critical part of a structured cabling system, and they provide the perfect pivot point for a network management system. The concept of a wiring hub has expanded and grown in the 1990s well beyond the first ARCnet wiring hubs, which brought together the coaxial cables and amplified and repeated signals. The early Ethernet 10Base-T and Token-Ring wiring hubs had the same basic level of functionality. Their primary job was to implement a physical star so that no electrical problem on one leg of the cable system would impact the entire network.

In the late 1980s, Synoptics and Cabletron raised the wiring hub to a new technological level that is practically an art form. Companies like Asante, David Systems, Digital Equipment Corporation, NetWorth, 3Com, Hewlett-Packard, and Optical Data Systems have joined SynOptics and Cabletron as major competitors in the hub business. Modern hubs are the home of powerful processors that run a variety of network utility and management programs, modules with connectors of every kind, and even routers and bridges that regulate network traffic. As Figure 5.1 illustrates, the wiring hub has evolved into the operational and physical center of the entire network.

Figure 5.1

This diagram shows a basic *premises distribution system* (PDS) that includes the "vertical" cabling between wiring closets, patch panels for the vertical cabling, both a chassis and a cabinet wiring hub, and a patch panel for the "horizontal" wiring going to the nodes.

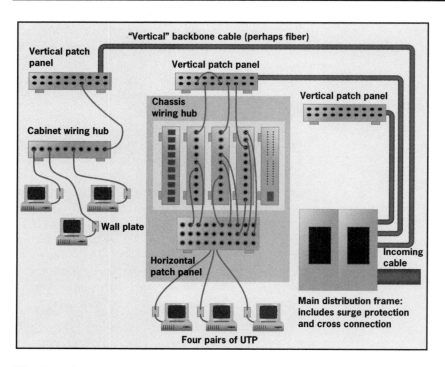

■ Cabinet and Chassis Hubs

Hubs generally fall into two categories that we refer to as cabinet and chassis. A *cabinet hub* is a single sealed cabinet with all of the connectors permanently attached and no internal expansion capability. These types of hubs are available for ARCnet, 10Base-T, and token-ring networks, but each hub only works for one type of network. Cabinet hubs are popular because of their low initial cost and small size. Used alone, they are appropriate for many installations, but you can also mix cabinet and chassis hubs on the same LAN to benefit from the low cost of the cabinet and the flexibility of the chassis.

A *chassis hub,* shown in Figure 5.2, consists of a metal cabinet with slots containing electrical connectors for add-in modules. The prime component of a chassis hub is an electrical backplane—a high-speed electrical path for data passing between the expansion modules. The backplane reduces the impact of the hub on the network cabling scheme, because data travels across the fast backplane instead of the slower LAN cable. Each cable connection module in the chassis cabinet is, in fact and in effect, a separate hub on the network, but the backplane removes both the 10Base-T three-repeater rule and the token-ring hub-to-hub cable factor from the cable equation. The backplane also improves overall network reliability, because it removes a vulnerable length of inter-hub cable from the physical system.

Figure 5.2

This chassis hub has slide-in modules that provide the flexibility to use different cabling schemes and networking schemes, to segment network cable systems, and even to add processors for routing and network management.

The add-in modules slide in from the front of the cabinet and make a force-fit connection to the connectors on the backplane. Each add-in module fulfills a specific purpose. You can order modules with a variety of network connectors for different types of cables, with internal electronics to match different types of network adapters, and with special functions such as packet routing and network management.

Many vendors make a variety of modules for their chassis hubs. You can select connection modules for any combination of cable and for any network architecture. There are various advantages to chassis hubs:

- Nodes connected by Ethernet over thick coax, Ethernet over thin coax, and Ethernet over UTP (10Base-T) can interoperate on the same network or on totally separate networks.

- Nodes connected by token-ring over UTP and by token-ring over STP can interoperate on the same network or on totally separate networks.

- Nodes connected by ARCnet over coaxial cable or by ARCnet over UTP can interoperate on the same network or on totally separate networks.

- Nodes using the same network communications protocols, such as IPX or IP, can exchange data through an internal router in the wiring hub, regardless of the type of cable or the network architecture they use.

- You can easily create new separate network segments as your system grows by changing a jumper or a switch.

Companies like Cabletron, NetWorth, Optical Data Systems, Synoptics, 3Com, and many others sell chassis hubs with a wide range of expansion capabilities and with features such as dual power supplies for added fault tolerance. Some companies such as Optical Data Systems even sell complete 486-based CPUs with megabytes of memory that slide into the chassis. The CPUs can run networking software, like Novell's NetWare, and typically perform as communications servers or routers—although they can even be file and print servers.

In our experience, only the smallest installations remain satisfied with a simple unexpandable cabinet hub. The only downside to chassis hubs is that they are several times more expensive on a per-port basis than equivalent cabinet hubs.

■ Differentiation through Management

The definitions of chassis and cabinet hubs seem to separate everything into two neat piles, but the real products don't distribute themselves as cleanly. Several vendors now make cabinet hubs that can connect to several different types of cabling—typically 10Base-T combined with AUI and a BNC for thin Ethernet. Vendors of cabinet hubs often offer some expansion capabilities in their products, including the ability to connect a group of so-called "stackable" cabinet hubs, shown in Figure 5.3, with a multiconductor cable that enables them to provide many of the same advantages as chassis hubs, but with lower up-front costs. However, vendors differentiate their hubs primarily through management capabilities.

Figure 5.3

These cabinet 3Com stackable wiring hubs gain chassis-hub flexibility through a backplane cable that links the hubs. Traffic between the hubs moves across the backplane cable instead of the network cable.

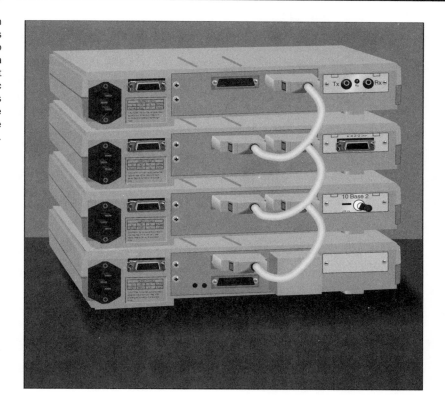

We aren't going to provide an exhaustive review of network management systems in this book on cabling. The information on cable testing and certification equipment in Chapter 9 is more important for cable installations than the larger topic of network management. But network management systems are tied to and rely on cabling systems. They can also help you in uncovering problems in the cabling system, so you should know a few of the facts and buzzwords.

There are several reasons to choose a wiring hub, either a chassis style or a cabinet style, equipped with a network management system, but all of the reasons hinge on gathering a baseline set of statistics that describe typical or normal performance and traffic load. This baseline of data allows you to quickly detect when and where things go wrong. If you first determine what is normal, then it is pretty easy to determine what is abnormal, and that's what a network management system is all about. The network monitoring and statistical reporting programs are like the level in the carpenter's tool-box—they indicate when operations are balanced correctly.

You can also use the set of baseline statistics to justify a budget for new equipment and software, to project personnel requirements, to bill clients and other departments for services, and to simply demonstrate the otherwise hidden role of the network in the organization's business. These statistics can help you make decisions about segmenting and augmenting the network based on the data gathered by the network management system.

After you determine the baseline data for your system, you set up network management *console* software that watches for and reports deviations from the baseline. Network management console programs can make database entries, generate network messages, and even dial your pager when they detect specific variations from the baseline. When a management program responds to a specific condition, that response is called an *alert*.

An alert is nothing more than a preprogrammed value for some parameter being monitored by the program. When the parameter—for example, the number of packets on the cable reaches the specified level (either abnormally high or low)—the program notifies something or somebody about the deviation. You can elect to set alerts for a wide variety of monitored parameters, ranging from the percentage of packet collisions to the number of packets coming from a specific server within the last minute.

Modern methods of communications and flexible software give these products more ways to sound an alarm than simply sending a message to a console operator. Network management products can dispatch a message to any networked PC, originate e-mail messages, or use a modem to dial the number of a pager service and even enter specific error codes for the pager's display. Monitoring programs can also execute other programs with their own scripted actions that can shut down processes, turn them on, and take a variety of other actions. In effect, you can monitor your network's problems from almost anywhere.

■ Network Management Architectures

In many modern organizations, the LAN carries the lifeblood of the operation and can often be as vital to production as the employees or the raw materials. Any downtime can have devastating consequences. The LAN deserves the benefit of a strong suite of management tools, and the wiring hub provides an excellent central point for network management. In structured network management systems, specific devices called *agents* communicate with a management program that collects and displays data. Software in the management station, typically a computer running UNIX or Windows, regularly polls the agents for their data, and agents can send alerts when they detect specific deviations from preset conditions. The three main sets of network management system standards (from least to most popular) are NetView, the Common Management Information Protocol (CMIP), and the Simple Network Management Protocol (SNMP). Figure 5.4 shows the possible locations of the agents on the network.

Figure 5.4

Network management agents, processors, and programs that collect statistical data are found in networked devices as varied as uninterruptable power supplies and routers.

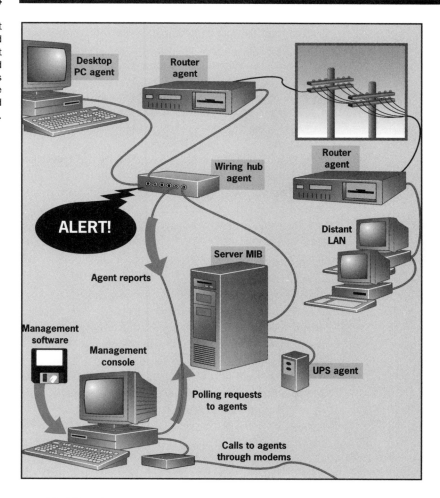

NetView is a management product developed by IBM and 3Com, and is generally the most expensive of the three systems to implement. This architecture requires extensive resources, including PCs and usually a mainframe, in order to operate. You'll typically only find NetView in "true blue" organizations running IBM hardware.

CMIP is an emerging "open" or widely published network management architecture that is gaining a lot of attention. It was developed by the International Standards Organization (ISO) and is now specified in U.S. federal government acquisitions. Because of the emphasis on an open architecture, CMIP offers the promise of operation across many different types of products and networks. The CMIP standard also describes a full-featured security system—something lacking in other management systems. But like many of the "open" standards, CMIP faces competition from older and proven standards that are backed by time-tested products such as SNMP.

SNMP, the most used and well-known of the current network management protocols, was defined by the Internet Engineering Task Force for managing networks based on the Transmission Control Protocol/Internet Protocol (TCP/IP). SNMP provides a common format by which network devices such as routers, wiring hubs, and bridges communicate defined sets of management data.

SNMP was first released in 1988 by the Department of Defense and the commercial developers of TCP/IP in an attempt to manage the different network topologies of complex internetwork systems. Since then, SNMP has grown into a widely accepted network management protocol, not just for interconnected networks, but also for smaller LANs using the same technology and topology. In May 1990, SNMP became a TCP/IP standard, which further increased its acceptance.

Agents and Consoles

All network management systems have basically the same architecture. Like Ethernet and ARCnet, the popular network management architectures differ in how they communicate across the network, but the concepts are basically the same.

The SNMP and CMIP standards each define a set of network management variables as well as the protocols or rules used to exchange network management information. In other words, the standard provides a common format for network devices and equipment such as bridges, concentrators, hubs, routers, and modems to send management data to the network management console software.

The agent typically consists of a special-purpose processor located in each SNMP or CMIP compatible piece of equipment—although it can simply be a program running in a multitasking environment like a file server. The generic term *management module* describes either the slide-in card used in a chassis hub or a processor built into a cabinet hub.

The management console software can run on a PC using Microsoft's Windows or on a UNIX-based workstation. The management console software polls each agent over the network cable for pertinent information regarding the individual nodes on the network, any error messages, and other statistics. It gathers the statistics from all agents on the network—there can be hundreds in a large LAN—and then presents the data in a useful format. Management console displays typically include multiple bar charts and graphs, and can provide various levels of real-time and historical data.

When the management console polls and controls the agents across the network cable, it employs *in-band* signaling—a term carried over from telecommunications systems. Management console actions initiated through a separate RS-232C port are described as *out-of-band* signaling. This type of signaling usually occurs during setup and from a remote PC through a modem.

Each agent stores information in a virtual database called a Management Information Base (MIB). The MIB stores all the information concerning traffic, equipment, and error logs. The MIB standard is constantly in evolution to increase the amount of available information and to further automate the management process. The agents can also send unsolicated information on high priority alerts.

One problem inherent in any protocol implemented by many different companies is compliance versus compatibility. Products can comply with a standard without being able to interoperate. Some vendors put proprietary information, called *extensions,* into the MIB. Software from other companies can't read these extensions, and errors result. Similarly, management software looking for proprietary extensions can't effectively display another vendor's agent equipment, so compatibility between agents and management console software from different companies is always a potential problem.

OpenView Management Software

The OpenView program, originated by Hewlett-Packard, is sold in slightly different forms by HP, Cabletron, and Synoptics. It is the basis on which all SNMP management console software is modeled. Cabletron and Synoptics have each separately changed some elements in the way the program stores and presents information, but all the programs have the same setup routines and operate identically to HP's OpenView.

All versions of the Windows package allow you to use a program called OVDRAW to pick icons to create a diagram of the network. However, the icons have been customized for each company's products. A program called OVADMIN allows you to customize the diagram to include details such as Ethernet addresses, concentrator names, and user names.

All of the programs display network traffic in the form of marching histograms and provide Windows boxes for error messages. You can set alarm levels for events, such as a certain number of collisions or bad packets, and set criteria for audit trails.

HP enhanced OpenView by adding a program that automatically attempts to "discover" SNMP agents on the network. While the company claims that OpenView works with any agent, our experience is that it can't always discover agents in hubs provided by other companies.

In their LattisNet Management Software, Synoptics divided the information into more screens than the other companies, but all screens are set up as separate windows in the Microsoft Windows environment, so you can choose and position the displays with a mouse. Synoptics also uses text files to set up the status of each SNMP agent node—not unlike a WIN.INI file. Cabletron's Remote LANView software uses a menu system that is easier to configure if you don't do it frequently.

■ Network Management and Troubleshooting

When the automated network management console reports an alert, the human troubleshooting sequence begins. The more information you have regarding normal operation, the quicker you can solve the problem of abnormal operation. If you know what the normal pattern of traffic and connections looks like, you can quickly spot problems. If you suspect the cable system is at fault, a wiring hub helps you to troubleshoot the problem by reporting stations with abnormally low traffic counts or with high levels of bad data. We describe more troubleshooting tips in Chapter 9, but the basic technique is no mystery to anyone who has ever tried to find the bad bulb in a string of Christmas lights: replace a suspect item with one known to be good. In the next chapter, we describe the wiring closet, patch panels, and other devices that help you troubleshoot and substitute cable segments.

- *Conduits and Raceways*
- *Up the Backbone*
- *In the Closet*

The Structured Cable System: Wiring Closets and Cross-Connections

The scout ship lurched violently and popped out of hyperspace too close to a star. "What have you done and why are we here?" Wirejack asked the ship.

"There is a malfunction in my central wiring core," the ship's voice replied in what was programmed to be an efficient and soothing manner. "I detected a discontinuity in the wiring core and dropped into normal space."

"Yeah, but it's too darn hot here," Wirejack moaned. "We're practically in the corona of that star. Get us out of here."

"I cannot access the normal space drive until the wiring discontinuity is repaired," the ship replied.

"Open the wiring core," Wirejack ordered.

The wiring core was the convergence of tens of thousands of individual meson beams sent by transceivers inside each discrete logic node in the ship. The transceivers twisted space and time so that the intersection was a fifth-dimension hole in the heart of the ship. In response to Wirejack's order, the ship created a normal-space portal into the fifth-dimension hole, and Wirejack gingerly inserted his head and one arm into the hole. His vision extended only a few inches, and he felt like he was pushing his hand through spider webs as it crossed the beams.

Then his fingers touched something solid. A worker at the last spaceport had left an alignment tool inside the hole, and it was floating around and interrupting the path of the beams. But when his fingers brushed against it, the tool drifted away. Wirejack was reaching as far as he could into the hole, and his breath was coming in gasps. His consciousness was fading as he tried over and over to grab the floating object.

"Willy? Willy? Are you okay?" Bill asked. Willy's hand brushed Bill's face and he grabbed it. Bill yelled, which startled Willy into letting go and simultaneously gasping in a deep breath of cool, conditioned air.

"Huh? What happened?" Willy asked.

"The heat in that darn wiring closet got to you," Bill replied. "It must be 120 degrees in there, and you were practically standing on your head trying to fish out that screwdriver I dropped into the cabinet. I had to pull you out."

The wiring closet in this job was poorly planned. It was the old broom closet of a remodeled building, but the remodeling hadn't included adding conduits to the walls or providing the wiring closet with air conditioning. The closet's only redeeming quality was its central location. The closet contained a wiring hub for 128 ports, a large, horizontal patch panel, a vertical patch panel, and an uninterruptable power supply for the hub. It was crowded and hot.

"Let's get a couple of fans," Willy said in a still-shaky voice. "We'll blow some air in there until we get those meson beams aligned."

Bill gave him a strange look while Willy drank some water and went back to find the dropped screwdriver.

Each wiring closet is a pulse point for a major network's cabling system, although many successful networks don't have even one wiring closet. In a small office, the total extent of the cable system can be a wiring hub hanging from the back of a desk with the cables running directly to the LAN adapters in each node. But in an installation of more than a dozen nodes, you'll want the flexibility of a wiring closet like the one shown in Figure 6.1. The equipment in a wiring closet typically includes patch panels for the vertical wiring, patch panels for the horizontal wiring, the wiring hubs, and other devices such as uninterruptable power supplies.

Figure 6.1

The wiring closet includes a variety of equipment including patch panels, wiring hubs, uninterruptable power supplies, and other devices such as modems and access servers. The vertical backbone cable and horizontal cable to the network nodes all terminate in the wiring closet.

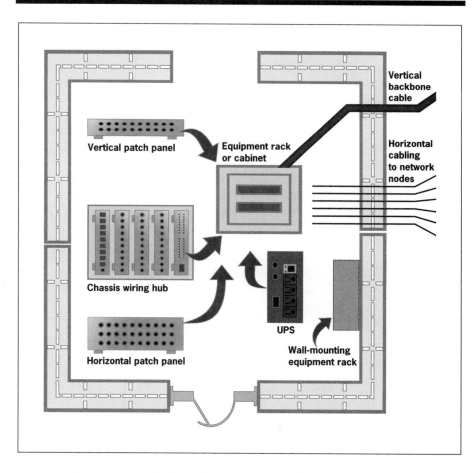

A wiring closet might be as big as a broom closet, or it might be part of a larger equipment room. On the one hand, a wiring closet should be easily accessible, but on the other hand, it is a vulnerable point in the network and should be well secured. A disgruntled employee or someone intent on mischief can disable your entire network during a few seconds' work in the wiring closet. Whether a wiring closet is a true closet or a part of someone's office, it should be physically secured.

In the ideal installation, each wiring closet is connected to a main cross-connect point—a series of panels with plug-in jumpers. The main cross-connection, also known as the main distribution frame (MDF), is often part of a larger server room containing communications servers, file servers, and perhaps even the desks of the people in the network management and support team. Of course, in many installations the main cross-connection is also the only wiring closet.

In this chapter, we describe the relationship of the wiring closets to the rest of a structured wiring plan, how to plan for the location and determine the size of a wiring closet, and the equipment inside the closet and their functions. We provide details of the various options associated with different network cabling schemes, for while most installations superficially look alike, they vary considerably in their specifics.

Generally, we also add some practical insights and observations to the recommendations made in three EIA/TIA standards:

- EIA/TIA-568: Commercial Building Telecommunications Wiring Standard

- EIA/TIA-569: Commercial Building Standard for Telecommunication Pathways and Spaces

- EIA/TIA-570: Residential and Light Commercial Telecommunications Wiring Standard

Note that as we go to press, the EIA/TIA is planning to replace these documents with a series of standards using an SP prefix. For example, EIA/TIA SP-2840 has been designated as the replacement for EIA/TIA-568. However, the technical descriptions are the same, and people will recognize the older descriptions and documentation for many years.

These standards are valuable additions to your technical library. You can obtain copies of these standards from:

Global Engineering Documents
15 Inverness Way East
Englewood, CO 80112
800/854-7179 or 303/267-1470

There is a substantial charge (approximately $50 to $100) for these documents.

HINT. *If your installer isn't familiar with these standards, get another installer.*

A comprehensive structured cable system like those designed by AT&T, Northern Telecom, Amp, Mod-Tap, and other companies provides a structured description of every inch of cable, every connector, and every additional piece of equipment in the cabling system. A structured cabling system begins with the cable connecting the wall jack to the LAN adapter. The wall-jack system (known in stuffier descriptions as the "telecommunications outlets") is an important part of the installation, because it must provide the correct electrical characteristics and be reliable through thousands of connections and disconnections. In addition to these requirements, it must also provide modularity so you can change between different cable options as your system evolves.

The cable that runs between each wall jack and the associated wiring closet is called the *horizontal wiring,* mainly to differentiate it from the so-called vertical wiring that forms the backbone between the wiring closets and the main cross-connect point in the building. Of course these are only general terms—the vertical wiring might actually be as horizontal as all the rest of the cabling, when compared to the horizon. The horizontal wiring is typically copper cable, while the vertical backbone wiring is often fiber-optic cable.

The specific equipment inside the wiring closet must meet the requirements of the specific type of network architecture such as Ethernet, ARCnet, token-ring, telephone, IBM 3270, or any of several wiring plans from Digital Equipment Corporation.

■ Conduits and Raceways

If you are fortunate enough to be working in a building that was designed to accommodate a network, you will probably have conduit—typically plastic pipes—going from each wall plate to the wiring closet and between the wiring closets. This conduit is both a blessing and a curse. On the positive side, if there is space left in the conduit, it should take you only a few minutes to pull a new cable, as a replacement for a bad one or for added capacity. New conduit should have a piece of string inside that an installer can use to pull the cable, and thoughtful installers find a way to get the string back into the conduit after a cable is pulled. A piece of equipment called a "fish tape"—a standard part of any installer's toolbox—consists of a reel of wire stiff enough to push its way through the conduit. The fish tape makes it easy to pull a cable.

On the negative side, no conduit ever has enough space. As needs evolve and installations grow, the number of cables usually grows to fill all the space in the conduit. The need to make the available space last as long as possible is a powerful argument in favor of unshielded twisted-pair and fiber-optic cable and a real mark against shielded twisted-pair.

If you aren't fortunate enough to have conduits in your walls, perhaps you at least have false ceilings and hollow walls that make it easier to run cable. When you plan the cable runs inside of ceilings and walls, here are a few rules to keep in mind:

- Always plan the cable arrangements so that copper data cables cross power lines at right angles. This approach limits the energy absorption and therefore the electrical noise on the data cable.

- Never run copper data cables parallel to 120 volt power lines at distances of less than 6 to 8 inches. Keep data cables at least several feet away from higher voltage power lines.

- Keep each copper data cable as far away as possible from sources of electrical noise, including fluorescent lights, motors, elevator relays, radio transmitters, microwave transmitters for burglar alarms, and anything else that consumes electrical power.

- Run the data cables by the most direct route. Every extra foot of cable used in a horizontal link to a wall plate can reduce the cable available for other horizontal links.

- If you have false ceilings, use cable hangers (there are many types of hooks, loops, and trays) to keep the weight off the ceiling tiles.

- Don't run UTP wires inside the same cable sheath for both data wires and voice telephone wires. The voice system will create spikes and crosstalk that disrupts the data system.

- Similarly, keep wires carrying data and those carrying voices on separate punch-down blocks.

- Don't bend cable tighter than a radius ten times the diameter of the cable.

- Patch cables pick up electronic noise, so keep the patch cables as short as possible.

- Strip off as little of the outside cable jacket as possible. If you strip off the outside jacket, particularly where wires enter conduit, the conductors can lie too close together and generate crosstalk.

In some solidly constructed buildings, you might not be able to run the cables inside the walls or ceilings. Panduit Electrical Group and other companies market products called *surface raceways* that house cables in a neat and rugged metal external ducts. Panduit also offers a series of data cables designed to run under carpeting.

■ Up the Backbone

Each wiring closet contains patch and cross-connect panels that connect to the horizontal wiring and to the vertical wiring, also known as the *backbone* wiring. In data installations, the wiring closet also houses one or more wiring hubs for the appropriate network architecture.

Vertical or backbone wiring, regardless of its actual orientation to the horizon, links each wiring closet to a main distribution frame (MDF), or cross-connect point. A separate cable runs between each closet and the main cross-connection. The function of the MDF is primarily to distribute circuits coming in from outside the building. The cross-connect panel in the MDF provides a testing and connection point for outside circuits and backbone wiring. The MDF cross-connect panel has terminations for the vertical cabling (which is often fiber-optic cable) that goes between wiring closets on different floors or in different work areas. Technically, the term "backbone" can include cabling between buildings.

The EIA/TIA standards specify that the backbone system should be a star configuration, with separate backbone cables going from the main cross-connect point to each wiring closet. While such a configuration is useful and expandable to a point, it eventually forces you into impractical scenarios, such as connecting a hub in a wiring closet on the 15th floor to a hub in a wiring closet on the 14th floor through the single cross-connect panel in the basement.

The standards allow for a second level of cross-connect points on the backbone. In the example cited above, you might put the second-level cross-connection on the 10th floor. But more importantly, the standards also allow for whatever separate direct connections are needed between each wiring closet. Technically, the direct connections between wiring closets are adjuncts to the backbone, but in practical installations these inter-closet connections are primary communications links.

Locating the Closets

As you plan for one or more wiring closets, you have to think in several dimensions. The parameters of your planning are defined by the maximum backbone cable lengths between each closet and the main cross-connection, by the maximum horizontal cable lengths between each closet and each wall jack, and by the maximum distances between wiring closets. It's like setting up a three-dimensional chess game with pieces of string. In this game, string of various lengths is tied to each chess piece and limits its position.

The game has other limitations, too, because each specific distance depends on the type of cable used in the cable span. On the backbone, for example, you get the best distance, as much as 6,560 feet (2,000 meters) from fiber-optic cable. Unshielded twisted-pair cable offers a maximum length of

2,624 feet (800 meters), while more complex rules apply to shielded twisted-pair and to Thick Ethernet coaxial cable.

Figure 6.2 provides some graphical examples of different cable combinations and how they impact the location of the wiring closets and cross-connect points. Use caution when examining Figure 6.2—the maximum cable lengths shown there are from the EIA/TIA standard. All of the Ethernet and token-ring specifications and limitations detailed in Chapter 4 still apply and, particularly in the case of token-ring, they are probably more limiting than the EIA/TIA standard.

Figure 6.2a

This diagram shows the maximum cable lengths allowed under the EIA/TIA-568 standard for four different types of cable. The most common combination uses STP for both the horizontal and backbone wiring, but fiber-optic cable is being used increasingly for the backbone.

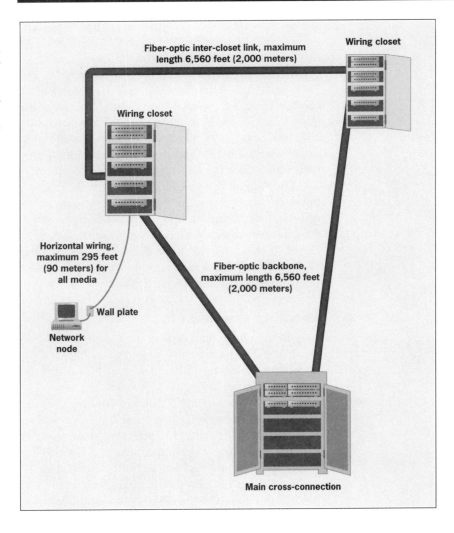

Figure 6.2b

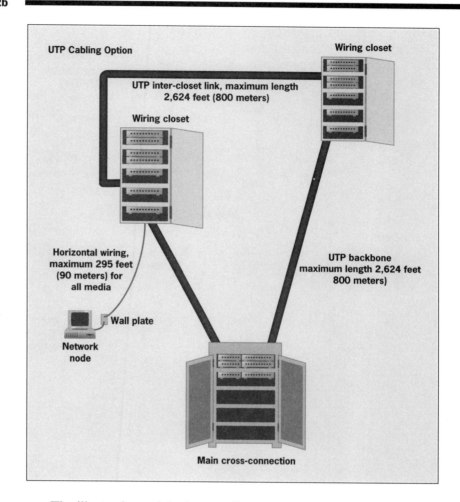

The illustrations of the intermediate cross-connect points in these diagrams can also be misleading. Where the diagram shows that inserting intermediate cross-connections provides longer runs, those intermediate cross-connect points would require repeaters or other devices to keep the entire system within the limitations of Ethernet or token-ring.

Finally, as you're planning the data cables, don't forget that the wiring closets and cross-connection points will need 120-volt AC power and good electrical grounds, too. Proper lighting, adequate heating, ventilation, and cooling should also be part of the plan.

Figure 6.2c

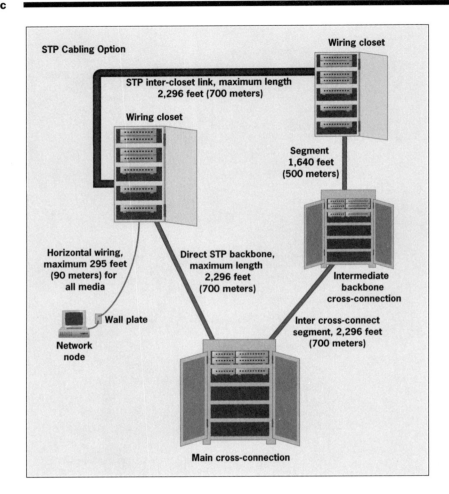

The Backbone Cable

Modern installations will typically use UTP or fiber-optic cable for the backbone. When the backbone is UTP, designers often select multipair cables. These cables are typically 25 pairs of 24 AWG wire. Each pair must have a different wire twist rate from all of the other pairs in the cable to reduce the crosstalk between the pairs. As explained in Chapter 3, the cable jacket must conform to the National Electrical Code, which means you'll often have to choose plenum-rated cable. We believe it's a good practice to select cable with UL markings. A variety of companies including AT&T, Anixter, and Belden make cable appropriate for use in the backbone.

Figure 6.2d

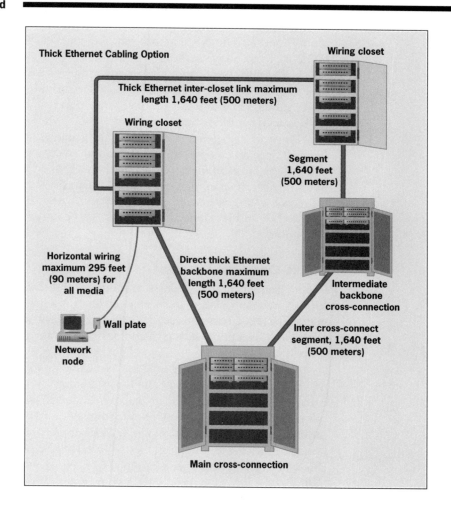

Fiber-optic cable used in the backbone is multimode, graded-index optical fiber with a nominal 62.5/125 micron core/cladding diameter. The same considerations concerning the fire rating of the cable jacket apply to fiber-optic cable.

■ In the Closet

The wiring closet holds a variety of equipment, and you have many options for how you configure it. The typical major pieces of equipment in a wiring closet are a backbone wiring cross-connect device, a horizontal wiring cross-connect device, patch cables, wiring hubs, and backup power for the wiring hubs. Increasingly, the wiring closet (which might be a large equipment room) also houses network portal devices such as a router, a cluster of modems, or an access server.

The wiring closet should never contain pipes carrying water, steam, or other liquids, the sole exception being a fire sprinkler system. Ideally, the closet shouldn't be used for other security, elevator, or heating and cooling purposes, or for other building services.

There are two general layouts for the equipment in a wiring closet: on the wall or in an equipment rack. Installers often combine both approaches and put the cross-connect devices on the wall while keeping wiring hubs and other devices in an equipment rack. The best finish for the walls inside a wiring closet is $3/4$-inch marine-grade plywood, rather than plasterboard. The plywood should be sanded, free of dust, and painted with a latex paint in a light color.

Cross-Connect Devices

People frequently change desks and offices, and their needs for connectivity evolve. Accommodating moves and changes is a major part of a network manager's job. Cross-connect devices make it easy to reconfigure the horizontal and backbone wiring to add network connections and to substitute for bad wire pairs.

A cross-connect device terminates a cable or a group of cables and makes the terminations available for interconnection to other cables. In typical data networks, one small cross-connect device will terminate the backbone cable and make it available for connection to a wiring hub. On the other side of the wiring hub, a larger cross-connect device will terminate the horizontal wiring before it enters the hub. These cross-connect devices enable you to easily adapt your cabling system to growth and, more importantly, to the moves and changes in your organization.

For about 30 years, the major type of cross-connection used in telephone systems was a *Type-66 block,* shown in Figure 6.3. This type of device, also known generically as a "telco splice block" or a "punch-down block," is still used, but it is under direct competition from modern alternatives that use modular telephone jack RJ-45 modular telephone jack connections.

The use of punch-down blocks for data connections is controversial. Some manufacturers claim that their punch-down blocks meet all criteria for impedance, attenuation, and crosstalk in data systems, but other experts express doubts that the mechanical connections will hold their quality over a long period of time.

Figure 6.3

The Type-66M punch-down block can terminate 50 pairs of wire. Each wire is "punched" into the jaws of a contact. The contact pierces the insulation to make the connection. Jumper wires placed between each contact make it easy to change connections to each network node.

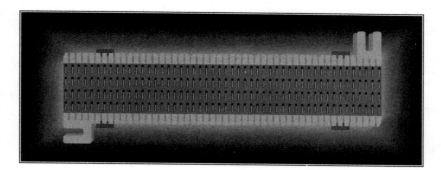

A punch-down block contains rows of terminals configured in a 10-by-3.44-inch or 1.25-inch-thick nylon or plastic package. Installers use a device called a *punch-down tool* to insert wires into the jaws of the terminals. The terminals pierce the insulation of the wire to make a connection. Typically, one 25-pair cable or a group of cables, such as the horizontal wiring, terminates on each punch-down block, and separate jumpers, often called *fly leads,* link the punch-down blocks. As needs and conditions change, installers can vary the jumpers to change the interconnections. Some punch-down blocks come prewired with a short, 25-pair cable and connector. The prewired connector is particularly useful for connections to a wiring hub.

The jumpers used between punch-down blocks present another set of problems. Installers must be careful to keep the leads twisted on the jumpers and to carefully dress the leads away from sources of electrical noise. Finally, the punch-down tool is a mechanical device that can cost $50 to $80, and installers need training and the patience to work with fine wires in this technical environment. Because of these drawbacks, alternatives to the punch-down block, such as the patch panel shown in Figure 6.4, are flourishing.

HINT. *Patch cables should always use stranded unshielded twisted-pair wire. We frequently see patch cables made out of flat silver satin or modular telephone cable that does not contain twisted wire. These patch cables are not acceptable, because they don't maintain the integrity of the cabling system.*

Krone, Inc. of Englewood, Colorado, markets a series of patch panels that terminate cable pairs in RJ-45 telephone jacks with four wire pairs per jack. The patch panel system is certified for Category 5 cable installations, and it can be mounted on a hinged wall mount or in a cable cabinet. One 19-by-7-inch panel can terminate as many as 96 connections. Preconfigured patch cables with RJ-45 connectors make it easy to alter configurations as needs change.

Figure 6.4

Moves and changes make life difficult for a network administrator. A patch panel provides a flexible and fast method of changing connections and adding services. For example, one strip of connectors might connect to the wiring hub through a 25-pair cable, while the other strip terminates the horizontal cables. Patch cables make the final link between the horizontal cable and the hub.

AT&T markets many versions of the AT&T 110 Connector System. The 110 Jack Panel System consists of 8-conductor RJ-45 jacks, mounted in a holder and wired to a block with terminating connectors. Panels are available in configurations with 12, 36, or 108 jacks, and you can combine panels to make huge installations. Similarly, Amp and Mod-Tap market cross-connect systems for practically any size network and any configuration. AT&T also offers PC software called the AT&T 110 Connector System Configurator that guides your planning for a single wiring closet or a complete building by posing a series of questions for you to work through.

HINT. *Some patch panels have RJ-45 connectors wired according to the AT&T 258A standards, and others are wired according to the EIA/TIA-568 standards. Be sure you know how your panels are wired and what kind of patch cord you have. Mohawk Wire and Cable is one of several companies offering special-purpose patch cables in their "Ultralink" product line.*

Octopus with a Harmonica

You'll find some strange things in the wiring closet—including an octopus attached to a harmonica. These odd devices connect various pieces of equipment. One common means of connection is a 50-connector jack, known generally as a "telco connector" or a 50-position modular jack, that terminates a 25-pair cable. In some cases, devices such as punch-down blocks and cross-connect panels come prewired with a telco connector and six feet of cable. In other cases, a 25-pair cable might break out into eight separate plugs, a configuration known as an "octopus." In other cases, the cable can terminate in a group of eight RJ-45 female jacks, a device known as a "harmonica." Figure 6.5 shows a hub with telco connectors.

Figure 6.5

A 50-pin "telco connector" is often used on wiring hubs and cross-connect devices to attach a 25-pair connecting cable. If the cable breaks out into individual RJ-45 plugs, it is known as an "octopus." If it terminates in a line of RJ-45 jacks, it is a "hamonica." You must carefully plan the number and gender of connecting cables you'll need in your wiring closet.

When you configure your wiring closet, you'll be faced with a variety of options concerning the use of octopus cables, harmonicas, double-ended telco extension cables, and devices such as wiring hubs and cross-connect panels equipped with telco jacks. It pays to draw a diagram and to create a list of parts so you can be sure of having the right kinds of cables and connectors on hand to finish the job.

Because the various manufacturers of wiring hubs and computer equipment offer models with different specifications, it also pays to know exactly what the manufacturers require and provide. For example, some manufacturers use female telco chassis jacks on their equipment, while others use male telco chassis plugs. Obviously, you must have the correct type of mating connector on the cable you use to link the equipment. To make matters worse, these 25-pair cable sets are typically prewired, and they are expensive. If you can't get advance information from individual manufacturers, Mod-Tap maintains a library of publications called "Mod-Tap Wiring Solutions" that document the exact installation recommendations of dozens of manufacturers.

Cabinets and Racks

Inside the wiring closet, patch panels and wiring hubs can mount on the wall in brackets, stand in racks, or reside in full cabinets that are racks with doors. Since the 1940s, electronic equipment has come in chassis with 19-inch-wide front panels, and cabling equipment is no exception. The mounting holes in these cabinets, spaced from $^5/8$ inch to 2 inches apart, match the holes in the front panels of the equipment. The popularity of this configuration means that you can choose from cabinets and mounting brackets made by many different companies. A few companies are marketing 23-inch wide products, but we recommend staying with 19-inch wide racks.

If you have a small installation, you should consider mounting the patch panels and wiring hubs on the wall using hinged wall brackets. These brackets are available in heights of $3^1/2$- to 14-inches high. A hinge on one side allows the assembly to swing out so you can work on the back side. This type of mounting uses space economically, but you must allow 19 inches for the panel to swing out from the wall. Some brackets come with a locking cover to deter tampering.

A distribution rack, like the one shown in Figure 6.6, is a simple skeletal frame, typically between 39 and 74 inches high, that holds 19-inch-wide equipment panels. The skeleton frame makes it easy to work on the front and back of the equipment. When you plan the closet, you should allow a 6-inch depth for the equipment and then another 12 to 18 inches minimum for physical access. Typically, a floor plate with a depth of about 22 inches provides stability and determines the minimum distance of the rack from the wall. You typically need a $^1/2$-inch socket wrench and an adjustable wrench to assemble a rack, and you should secure the rack to the floor in some way.

A full equipment cabinet, shown in Figure 6.7, is much more expensive than a distribution rack, but it offers the advantage of security because you can lock the cabinet doors. A typical equipment cabinet is 72 inches high, 29 inches wide, and 26 inches deep. A cabinet requires at least 30 inches of clearance in front to allow the door to swing open. Some fancy cabinets have Plexiglass doors through which the lights of modems and other devices are visible.

South Hills Datacomm and Newton Instrument Company are retailers of wiring closet brackets, racks, and cabinets that offer a wide inventory of products.

Figure 6.6

A distribution rack is a simple frame that holds equipment with a standard 19-inch front panel width. Racks provide flexibility and are only moderately expensive.

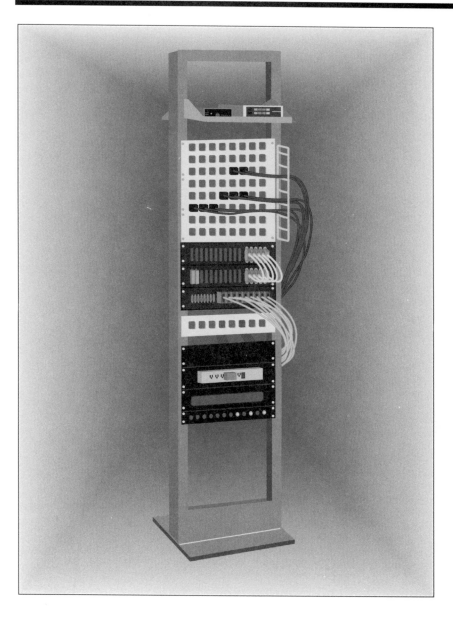

Figure 6.7

An equipment cabinet provides added security, but it requires more space—including room for the door to swing open.

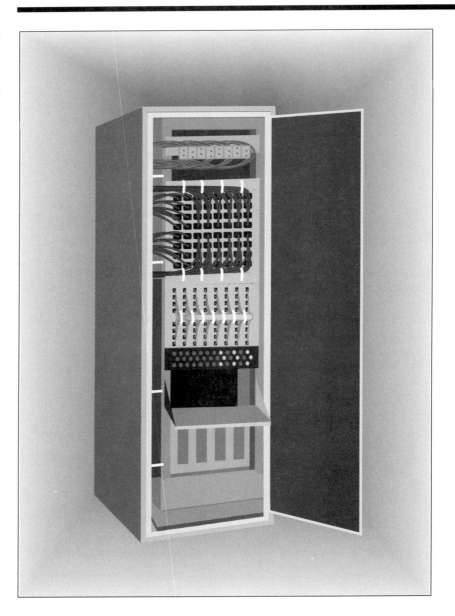

Neat Cables

Neatness counts! You are judged by how your wiring closet looks, and for good reason. The cables emerging from the conduits or racks must be arranged neatly to avoid damage to cable pairs and to simplify adding cables and troubleshooting. Before the 1970s, cables were bound together using waxed twine. The ability to neatly sew cables together with twine and a needle was highly prized among cable installers. Replacing a cable often meant discarding many feet of neatly sewn twine.

During the 1970s, several companies made available self-locking cable ties, shown in Figure 6.8. These ties come in many sizes and materials. Installers can quickly whip a tie around a group of cables and lock them tightly together. Best of all, if you have to make repairs you can quickly snip off the necessary cable ties.

Figure 6.8

Cable ties are an installer's best friend. Plastic cable ties hold cables securely and speed installation. In addition, they easily break apart for additions and repairs.

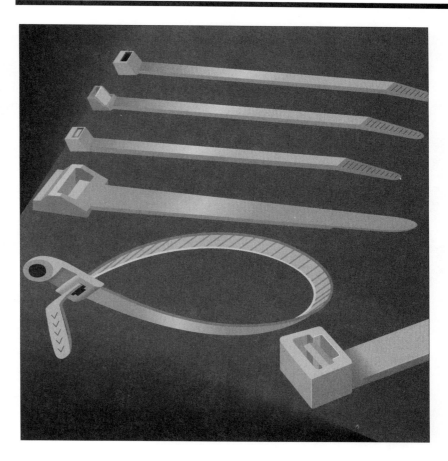

HINT. *You can never have enough cable ties. Buy them by the dozens in big sizes—you can always cut off the excess. Some cable ties come with screw mounts, so you can secure them to a wall. Companies also offer special adhesive mounts with a hole for the wire tie.*

In addition to being neat, your cables should also be clearly identified. You can buy identification tags for the cable ties or use separate slip-on or adhesive labels for the cables. EIA/TIA standard 606 (Administration Standard for the Telecommunications Infrastructure of Commercial Buildings) describes a method of numbering and labeling cabling, pathways, and spaces. The 606 standard recommends specifically colored tags for different types of cables. For example, network connections are green, backbone cables are white, and horizontal cables are blue.

Frankly, few installations require the complex specifications of the standard, but you should have some reasonable method of identifying each cable pair and piece of equipment. At least, every cable should be labeled at each end.

Uninterruptable Power Supplies

Your wiring closet needs an uninterruptable power supply (UPS). It does no good to equip network file servers with backup power and then to allow the wiring hubs to go without power during a power failure. Wiring hubs don't require much power, but if you have other devices in the closet like a router or access server, you'll need more capacity. You must base the UPS selection on the power requirements of the equipment in the wiring closet.

Product features in the UPS market are often obscured by marketing techno-babble. For example, some vendors rate the capacity of their units in volt amps (VA) and others rate their units in watts. The difference between ratings in volt amps and in watts is as much a matter of marketing as of technology. In a marketing sense, a small UPS device can be said to put out more VA than watts. In a technical sense, the VA system is more accurate, because the true maximum output of the UPS is limited by its output current capacity, which is directly related to the VA rating.

In resistive devices, such as light bulbs, the voltage and current are in phase, and the device makes full use of power applied. But when devices show an inductive or capacitive component to the power line—and most electrical devices do—the voltage and current get out of phase, and the devices don't make the most efficient use of the applied power. A number called the *power factor* describes the phase relationship. The power supplies in PCs typically have a power factor of about 0.6.

To further complicate the math, a PC's power supply is only about 75 percent efficient. It loses about 25 percent in heat and fan noise. The power supply wattage number that you'll find in the typical documentation for a

PC shows the power supply output, not its input. The required input is considerably higher.

Here is an example applying the 75 percent efficiency and 0.6 power factor to a PC showing a 200-watt power supply. The bottom line demonstrates the method of finding the appropriate VA rating of a UPS:

PC Watts $=$ 200 watts (manufacturer specification)
PC Input Watts $=$ 200 $\div$ 75% efficiency $=$ 267 watts
PC Input VA $=$ 267 $\div$ 0.6 power factor $=$ 445 VA

HINT. *As a quick rule of thumb, you should choose your UPS with a VA rating at least two times the combined wattage ratings of all the power supplies that the UPS will support.*

Connections up and down the Line

Although a wiring closet might not always be a closet, it will always be one of the most important parts of the network. The patch panels and cross-connect points in the wiring closet make it easier for you to expand and reconfigure the network and can save many times their initial cost in the wall wrecking, rebuilding, and reconstruction you will otherwise need to do later. It costs more to do it right the first time, but when your business depends on its network connections, it pays to install it correctly the first time.

- *Where Problems Can Begin*
- *What Is a Ground?*
- *Grounding Problems*
- *Normal Mode and Common Mode Power Problems*

7

Power Wiring and Grounding

"Let's get started!" The woman calling the meeting to order wasn't here to socialize. As the men sitting around the table fell silent, all of them felt a cold icicle of doubt. Each man was sure his part of the system was working right, yet somehow glitches kept occurring. This was a big job, and there was a lot of money—invisible but vulnerable—on the table.

"I've never been involved in such a finger-pointing game!" Cheryl Hudson exclaimed. "According to each of you, nothing's wrong, yet nothing works. I've held up final payment on the master contract, and none of you gets another dime until this computer system works. Now who wants to start?"

A large man dressed in a T-shirt and sitting at the end of the table spoke up first. "Well, I know it's not my program. That's proven code! I demonstrated it for you at our offices and it works fine."

"The problem acts like a software bug," Cheryl replied, "but yes, the software does seem to work in demonstrations on different computers in different places. So is the problem in the computer hardware?"

This raised the hackles of a smaller man in a shiny suit. "No way! We've run the software on those same computers we fabricated in our gara...umm... I mean in our offices and it works fine. The problems start when the computers are brought into this building."

"Willy, does it come down to the cabling?" Cheryl asked the man dressed in a white shirt with "OK Cable" stenciled on the left pocket.

"I'd still be out there checking if I wasn't so certain," Willy responded. "But I've got attenuation, spectrum noise, and crosstalk readings on every LAN cable in your building. After you reported the first problems, we went back and checked everything twice. This is a great cable installation." He waved his hand for emphasis at the pile of printouts showing graphs and tables of numbers. "But I'll admit," he continued, "that's it's really curious how the hardware and software stop working when they come together in this building. I'd say you're missing two people in this meeting—a priest and an electrician."

Cheryl eyed him like he'd spent too long smelling the fumes from hot solder, while the others seemed vaguely relieved that the guilt might splatter on someone, anyone, else.

"Either this place is haunted or it has a power problem," Willy continued. "If you want to eliminate all of the options, you need to look into both of those possibilities, too. But, uh, I think the power problem is more likely."

The others were silent, but Cheryl said, "Wait a minute. This is a new building, the lights don't blink, and everything seems to run fine. How could we have a problem with the power?"

"You can have many kinds of power problems in new and old buildings. There is one kind of power problem called third-order harmonics that can affect a computer system despite filters on the power supply. It can cause intermittent outages that look like software problems. You have a big building fed

by several separate transformers, which creates the potential for a couple of different types of power problems."

The meeting broke up after Willy gave Cheryl the telephone number of a consulting engineer who specialized in analyzing commercial power systems. He kept the priest's telephone number in his pocket.

Cheryl never called back, and Willy figured that no news was good news. Three weeks later, when the final check for the cable installation work arrived in the mail, he called her. "We had another one of those tense meetings in that same room," she explained, "but this time it was between the engineer you recommended, the power company, and electrical contractor. I didn't understand a word they said beyond 'neutral to ground connection.' The electrician didn't admit to anything, but there was a crew working on the power panels the next morning, and after they left at noon the computer system ran just fine."

"Yeah, Cheryl," Willy replied with a smile in his voice, "but the full moon is this week. That will be the real test."

There are only a few things you need to know about power and grounding, but they are important enough to merit their own chapter because WHAT YOU DON'T KNOW COULD KILL YOU. If you become involved in network cabling and ignore grounding, you could set up situations in which lethal voltages exist between different pieces of computer equipment. In less dramatic circumstances, you could create installations in which the network is subject to frustrating, intermittent, and mysterious failures due to AC power and grounding problems. These problems fall into several categories, but they all occur because of bad design or bad connections.

■ Where Problems Can Begin

AC power-line noise is everywhere inside buildings. A sensitive oscilloscope displays AC power-line noise on its screen when you wave the probe in the air. Engineers design the computer data bus to siphon AC line noise to a neutral ground, but a designer can only do so much while also trying to accommodate low-power, fast data signals. In some instances, AC line noise coupled from a nearby video monitor or hard disk drive can create errors in a computer system, because it literally buries the desired signals and prevents logic gates from detecting the leading and trailing edges of the square waves. The problem is compounded if the computer has a poor ground connection.

Other problems related to power and grounding result from *electrostatic discharge*—the arc that jumps from your fingertips when you walk over certain materials in cool dry air. A static discharge can shoot through your computer like a bullet, destroying semiconductors and data in a seemingly random manner. Good grounding can eliminate the threat from electrostatic discharge.

■ What Is a Ground?

In both alternating current and direct current systems, electrons flow from the negative source, such as a battery or generator, to the positive source. A complete circuit with two conductors is required to carry the flow of electrons. In earlier commercial power systems, the earth was one half of the circuit. At the beginning of the 20th century, electrical power was delivered to homes and offices over just one wire (see Figure 7.1). The return path was through the earth itself, which acted as an electrical ground. Copper poles driven into the ground at the power transmitting station and at the home or business grounded the negative side of the circuit. The electrons moved through the moisture of the soil.

However, the earth has a high resistance to electrical flow, and as the consumption of power increases, the loss of power in the earth makes the one-wire system impractical. The one-wire power system quickly gave way to one that delivered power using two copper wires. This system, still used in some countries, is more efficient, but a problematic current path often still exists through the earth between the device using the electricity and either the generating plant or its nearest electrical supply point, typically an electrical transformer.

All modern electrical distribution systems send power across open spaces and across towns at very high voltages. A transformer, shown in Figure 7.2, reduces the high transmission voltages to the 120 or 240 volts used in consumer electronic equipment. The transformer can have several windings that feed separate legs of the electrical system. The transformer is your computer's interface to the commercial power grid.

The difference in the resistances between the copper wire path and the earth path can cause a voltage difference to exist between the cabinet or case of an electrical device and the earth ground. This voltage difference can become lethal if one wire going back to the power transformer has a poor connection and the earth ground provides a connection with a lower resistance. The voltage difference can create an electrical shock in extreme cases, and can cause other damage such as galvanic corrosion in less-serious situations. Since an earth ground can be something as simple as a wet floor or a water pipe, it's too easy for people to touch the case of a piece of electrical equipment and receive a shock if the equipment is fed with a two-wire electrical system.

Figure 7.1

Early electrical power delivery used one wire and grounded the current in the soil.

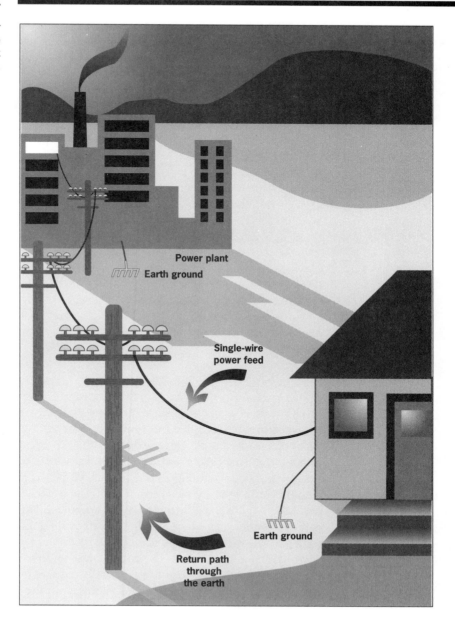

Power plant

Earth ground

Single-wire power feed

Earth ground

Return path through the earth

Figure 7.2

A power transformer reduces the high voltages used to overcome distance to voltages appropriate for electrical service. Transformers can have multiple secondary stages used to feed several homes or offices. Equipment on the same secondary stage can create electrical interference even though it is in a different building.

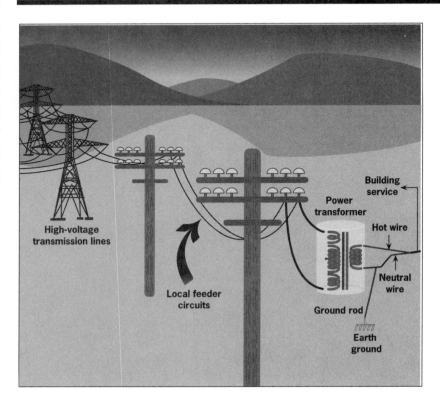

Modern power systems use three wires. The two wires that come from the transformer are called the "hot" wire and the "neutral" wire. The neutral wire is connected to an earth ground at the power plant and at the local transformer. In North America, the neutral wire is connected to the longer vertical slot (shown in Figure 7.3) in the AC power socket, and the hot wire is connected to the shorter vertical slot. The third wire in the AC power system, which is accessed through the round hole in North American power sockets, connects to a local earth ground for the building. The power plug connects this wire to the outside case of electrical equipment to ensure that no voltage potential exists between the case and the earth ground.

Unfortunately, a large building typically requires more than one so-called earth ground, and the earth ground is almost never the same between two buildings. If the ground wires in two separate locations have slightly different potentials to the common and hot leads, then there will be a voltage difference between the chassis of the equipment in the two locations. This usually isn't a problem, because someone would need very long arms to reach between devices with different ground connections. However, a network cable can connect such devices.

Figure 7.3

In the North American AC power connector, the neutral wire connects to the longer vertical slot, the hot wire connects to the shorter slot, and the wire going to a local building ground connects to the round hole.

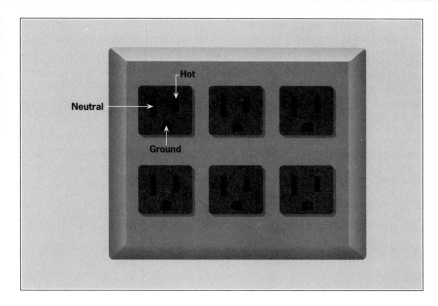

If a system works correctly, there should be no voltage difference between a network cable and the chassis of a computer. The IEEE 802.X committees were careful to create standards that isolate the LAN cable connections from the power connections. Unfortunately, things don't always work as planned.

If a building has faulty wiring—particularly a faulty ground wire connection to an outlet—lethal voltages can exist between the LAN cable and the chassis of a piece of equipment. Even plugging the LAN cable into the network interface card doesn't solve the problem because, according to the standard, the interface card's connection is isolated from the chassis power ground. Putting your hand on the computer's chassis and touching an Ethernet T-connector can result in a dangerous shock if the AC wiring has a problem. Similarly, dangerous voltages on RS-232 or parallel printer cables can occur if the pieces of equipment on either end are plugged into power circuits with different ground connections.

Because electricity doesn't travel over glass, we strongly recommend using fiber-optic cables to link buildings as well as wiring closets on different floors, particularly if the buildings or floors are fed by different power transformers. Also, fiber-optic cables don't carry lightning strikes between buildings, which commonly cause damage on campus-wide networks.

◼ Grounding Problems

Engineers designing digital systems need what is called a *signal reference ground* to establish the reference point for the 3- or 5-volt data signals inside the computer and to drain off leaked AC power. This signal reference ground must be close to the digital circuits, so engineers design a *ground plane,* typically a large area of conductive material, into circuit boards and use the computer equipment cabinet as a common point of connection for the circuit board ground planes to establish the signal reference ground.

In an ideal world, the signal reference ground would be completely isolated from the electrical ground. In the massive computer rooms installed in the 1960s, the signal ground system was an elaborate web of conductors under an elevated floor supporting the equipment. An isolated signal ground keeps AC power leakage and voltage spikes off the electrical ground. But in the real world of engineering, computer design, and compromise, the chassis of an electronic computing device serves as both the signal reference ground and the AC power line ground. It simply isn't practical to design modern PCs and other devices with a signal reference ground that is insulated from the power ground.

This link between the signal reference ground and the power ground means that problems with the power ground can interfere with the data system. Power grounding problems fall into two basic categories: an open or high resistance ground, or an abnormal pulse or condition between power conductors. But signal grounding problems are more complex.

Open or highly resistive power grounds occur primarily because of poor installation, vibrations that loosen connectors, or corrosion. These are simple but potentially dangerous problems that can be detected by a relatively low cost AC circuit tester, like the one shown in Figure 7.4, which measures the voltage difference between the neutral wire and the ground wire at an electrical socket. Typically, a set of lights on these devices indicates proper connections. A tester like this is a good investment in safety for anyone with wiring and cabling responsibilities.

But those testers do not uncover signal ground problems. Electrical contractors typically don't care about the length of the neutral and ground wires feeding each power outlet, but these long wires act as an antenna for electrical noise that interferes with higher frequency data signals. The safety provided by the AC ground wire connected to the chassis is a critically important factor, but it can lead to problems with more sensitive data signals.

Figure 7.4

An AC circuit tester is a relatively simple device, available through hardware stores and speciality tool companies. It can indicate problems with any of the three wires in an AC power outlet.

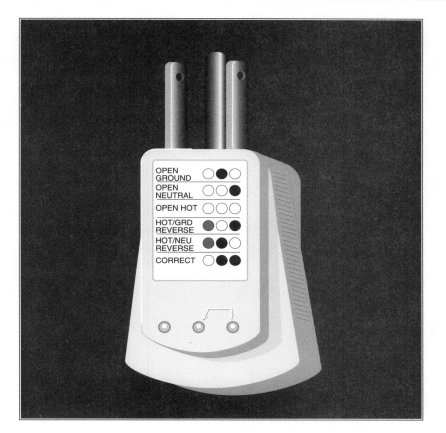

Generally, the best advice we can provide is to work closely with your electrical contractor and the power company to get the best and shortest electrical ground you can afford, as illustrated in Figure 7.5. In a small network installation, you can investigate the costs of getting a single power transformer dedicated to your office. If you have your own transformer, you can control the attachment of other devices, such as motors or high-current electrical heaters, that can generate electrical noises.

You should ask your electrical contractor to provide separate power distribution panels, normally known as *breaker boxes,* for each office area. The neutral wires and the ground wires from each outlet come together in the breaker box, so you have a better chance of shortening the effective length of the signal ground if each office has its own breaker box.

Figure 7.5

If you have your own power transformer, you can control the devices connected to your leg of the power circuit. Installing individual power distribution panels for every cluster of computers increases the up-front cost of power wiring, but it reduces the length of the ground wires and can limit several kinds of disruptive electrical noise.

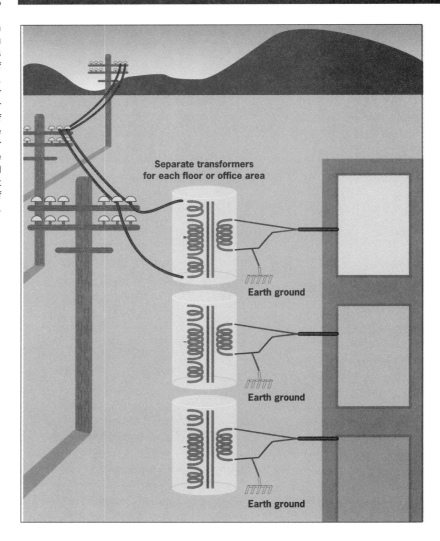

Separate transformers
for each floor or office area

Earth ground

Earth ground

Earth ground

■ Normal Mode and Common Mode Power Problems

Open or highly resistive ground connections can cause serious safety problems and difficult data problems, but other conditions on the power line can cause additional categories of mischief. These conditions can be shorts between wires on the power line or power fluctuations called surges, spikes, or sags that appear between the power conductors.

There are three wires in the power cable, and power problems can be classified according to which wires they effect. If a condition exists between the hot and neutral conductors, it is called a *normal mode* problem. If a condition involves either the hot or neutral conductors and the ground, it is referred to as a *common mode problem.*

Normal mode problems are usually intercepted by a computer's power supply, an uninterruptable power supply, or an AC power-line filter. Because common mode problems can go directly to the computer chassis without an intervening filter, they can do more insidious damage to data signals than normal mode problems—and they are harder to detect.

Spikes, Surges, and Sags

The most typical problems coming across the power lines are the voltage surges, sags, and spikes. Each type of power surge or loss has its own name based on its characteristics: the amount of voltage it imposes on the power lines and its duration. The majority of these events appear as normal mode problems—they enter between the hot and neutral lines. But incorrectly connected wiring or the physical failure of connectors or equipment can cause them to appear as common mode problems—usually with more disasterous results.

A *spike* or impulse refers to an overvoltage, superimposed on the desired line voltage waveform, lasting between 0.5 and 100 microseconds and possessing an amplitude over 100 percent of peak line voltage. In simpler terms, this means your power line has been struck with a short-duration but powerful hit of at least 240 volts.

You have a *surge* on the power line when the voltage reaches above 110 percent of the nominal value. A surge typically lasts only seconds, but this type of disturbance accounts for nearly all hardware damage experienced by small computer users. Most computer power supplies running at 120 volts cannot handle 260 volts for any length of time.

Other possible power disturbances include sags and oscillations. A *sag,* or brownout, occurs when the power-line voltage falls below 80 percent of the nominal value and lasts several seconds. An *oscillation,* also referred to as harmonics or noise, is a secondary signal on top of the 60-Hz waveform with a magnitude ranging from 15 to 100 percent of the nominal line voltage. Complex building wiring systems, particularly those that load many different legs onto power transformers, and unwanted interconnections between the neutral and ground wires are common causes of oscillation.

Oscillation is best cured by rewiring to get the most clean and direct power and ground connections you can afford. Sags and complete power outages are handled by uninterruptable power supply systems. Spikes and surges are caught by surge suppressors.

Surge Suppressors

The typical surge protectors that mount on a wall power socket have circuitry designed to protect the connected computer system from spikes and surges. The most common method they employ today is a metal oxide varistor (MOV). This device protects the equipment by diverting excess voltages to a ground. However, recent research at the National Institute of Standards and Technology indicates that the commonly used divert-to-ground scheme can still result in damage to data and equipment. Because it's the common reference point for data going into and out of the computer, dumping spikes and surges into the power-line ground close to the computer can create its own problems. Although the diversion to the power-line ground can avoid damage to the power supply, it can still garble the data.

Surge suppression devices that dump large quantities of voltage onto the common ground can create a large voltage differential between the nodes on the network, which can result in data loss or fried input circuits on the computers and printers exposed to the redirected surge. Another limitation stems from the MOV's limited in-service lifetime, which depends upon heat, usage, and other factors.

We suggest that you work with your electrical contractor to install commercial quality surge protection at each power distribution panel, as shown in Figure 7.6, instead of buying individual surge protectors for each networked device. Placing the surge protector at the office power panel doesn't reduce its effectiveness, but it does reduce the impact of voltage surges and spikes that are routed to the ground circuit.

Uninterruptible Power Supplies

Low voltage conditions (sags) and voltage interruptions are cured by uninterruptible power supplies. In their marketing literature, the UPS companies bury you in brownouts, whip you with waveforms, and petrify you with power factors. Many people who need an uninterruptible power supply are frightened off by the conflicting buzz of technical phrases, claims, and concepts that UPS vendors wrap around their products. No other part of the computer market seems to threaten you with such total disaster if you don't select the right product. Fortunately, the truth is much simpler.

Local area networks need the support of uninterruptible power supplies; every network file server absolutely requires power backup. If you use powered wiring hubs, you must provide backup power for the wiring hubs, too. Extended networks with bridges and routers need power backup to avoid systemic failures. Smart network administrators also know they must supply backup power for LAN client stations, because it does users little good to have an operational server and wiring system if their computers go down before they can save their spreadsheets and word processing files.

Figure 7.6

When you install
separate power
distribution panels for
each office or cluster of
computers, you should
also install surge
protection devices at the
power panels.

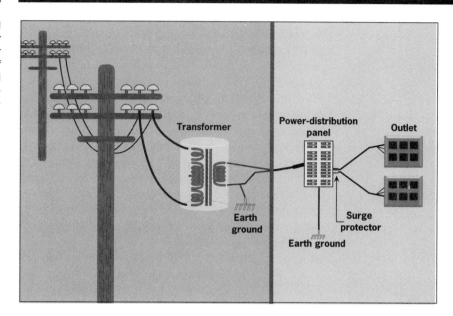

Today's desktop computers have robust and durable power supplies able to survive an amazing gauntlet of brownouts and interruptions. Many UPS companies expend a lot of effort convincing you that pure sine wave power works better for computer power supplies than other waveforms. Some devices with older-technology power supplies or motors running directly from the AC line do run better on sine waves, but modern desktop computers thrive on square waves, trapezoidal waves, or any other kind of alternating current waves you feed them. However, if you plan to back up printers with a UPS, the circuitry in many printers clearly prefers pure sine waves to their more-jagged cousins.

Frankly, while most of the claims and specifications broadcast by UPS vendors are important to purists, they shouldn't concern someone who wants backup power for network devices. Buyers need to know two things: First, will the UPS provide power to the network devices through most outages; and, second, will the UPS tell the servers it's about to run out of juice and initiate an orderly shutdown of the system?

Two separate studies conducted by IBM and Bell Laboratories investigated the type and nature of power disturbances. The studies revealed that more than half of all power disturbances last less than 6 seconds; they also found that power disturbances occur on the average of twice a week for most commercial sites.

Power outages fall into two categories: a few minutes and a few hours. Outages lasting a few minutes take place when something—a lightning strike, an unfortunate squirrel, or a wayward mylar balloon—creates a power line overload that trips a circuit breaker. Since these circuit breakers possess automatic reset capabilities, they can work from the surrounding power grid in to the source of the short to reestablish power within seconds or minutes.

Outages of several hours' duration take place when something—a car crashing into a power pole, a fire, or high winds—physically disrupts the power transmission system. This kind of outage typically lasts for hours or until repair crews can restore service.

If you require absolutely uninterrupted power, even during outages of several hours, then you need a generator to supplement your UPS, rather than an extremely large UPS. But if you just wish to survive the typical short-duration interruption and have time to gracefully shut down the system when short outages become long outages, then you only need a few minutes of UPS power. Almost all of the UPS units on the market support a heavily equipped server for more than ten minutes.

The typical UPS consists of a set of batteries, a battery charger, and a power inverter. The inverter does the job of converting the relatively low, direct-current voltage of the batteries into the typical 117 volts of alternating current normally supplied by the power line. It's difficult to produce pure sine-wave power from an inverter, because an inverter creates alternating current by switching the direct current from the batteries on and off quickly. Changing these pulses into pure sine waves takes a lot of circuitry. The battery charger keeps the batteries in peak condition during normal operation from the power line.

Simply stated, big batteries let UPS systems provide more power for a longer period of time. The amount of output power and the output duration increase or decrease in an inverse ratio. All modern UPS products use sealed, maintenance-free batteries. Like ordinary automobile batteries, the batteries are all based on some form of lead-acid technology, often incorporating a gelled electrolyte for added safety so that the active chemical agent doesn't spill or vent hazardous fumes.

UPS products differ primarily in the power storage capacity of the batteries, the power delivery capability of the inverter, the waveform output of the inverter, and whether the inverter operates all the time or only when the input voltage reaches a specific low or high level. Full-time systems require robust components and designs, and therefore cost more money. Minor differences between products include the indicators they provide to signal the status of battery life and power load, and the aural and visual alarms they use to alert you to problems.

Not all UPS products work identically. Most of the low-cost products act as standby power systems (SPSs). They monitor the power line and, if a problem occurs, switch in the inverter, powered by their batteries. The time needed to switch from power line to battery-supplied power, called the transfer time, can be just a few milliseconds. Meanwhile, the power supplies in modern desktop computers can coast for at least a hundred milliseconds without causing a system failure.

The on-line UPS design, typically more expensive, constantly supplies power from the inverter while the batteries continue charging from the the AC power line. No spikes or noise pulses from the power line reach the supported PC, because the inverter supplies freshly generated alternating current. When the AC line faults, the battery smoothly supplies power to the inverter. The protected device never experiences a millisecond of outage, and the transfer time is nil.

Some products appear to be on-line systems because they can adjust to low voltages without switching to battery backup, but, like SPSs, they don't run their inverters all the time. These devices use a ferroresonant transformer design that regenerates the sine wave for a more stable voltage and an output free of distortions. Products with ferroresonant designs offer excellent line-filtering capability with virtually no switching time. These systems fall into a hybrid UPS category.

The UPS supporting a network server must communicate with the server and warn it to close files and shut down when its battery power nears its end. Most UPS-to-LAN interface programs also report when the server starts to run on battery power and notify any network client stations fortunate enough to be up and running after the outage.

Apart from the necessary power cord connection, the method of connecting the UPS to the server varies. Most vendors supply you with an appropriate interconnecting cable and software on request so that you can monitor the UPS. However, you must carefully decide what kind of cable and software you need for your hardware and operating system combinations.

Underwriters Laboratory (UL) has a safety standard covering uninterruptible power supply equipment. In Canada, the Canadian Standards Association (CSA) performs the same function. UL standard 1778 describes exactly what a UPS is and does. UL testing stresses the safety of products, and only products that pass specific UL testing procedures can carry the UL seal. Many state and federal agencies and private corporations require products they buy to carry UL approval. We believe that UL or CSA approval should be an important consideration when you buy a UPS.

UPS protection, combined with the other power and grounding recommendations illustrated in Figure 7.7, will keep your network safe and reliable. Power wiring is just as critical to good network performance as the network cable—in the end, both safety and the performance of the computer system are at stake.

Figure 7.7

Using dedicated power transformers, separate power-distribution panels, surge protection, and uninterruptable power supplies in a distributed network

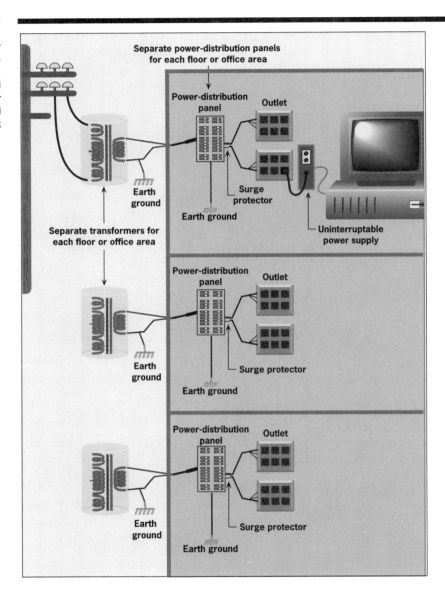

You should buy UPS protection for every network server, wiring hub, and bridge or router on the network. Since you don't need to buy excessively large and expensive products, you can afford to back up many networked desktop computers, too. Relying on a few criteria such as UL approval, the right network interface, and appropriate sizing, you can confidently ignore the technobabble and choose from among many fine products in the market.

- *Information Outlets*
- *The Station Cable*

From the Wall to the Desktop

"We went a full year without a single major problem. Now, within the last 30 days, we've got a rash of what seem to be cabling problems, but they're intermittent. I'm stumped, Willy."

"Okay, Margaret, let's see what we can find." Willy intended to plug a cable analyzer into the wall jack to measure the noise and crosstalk on the cable segment between the wall and the wiring closet. But when he disconnected the station cable running from the desktop to the wall jack, something didn't feel right. "This RJ-45 jack is kinda sloppy. OK Cable didn't make up your station cables, did we?"

"No, our maintenance staff made those cables after you were done with the installation job," Margaret replied.

"Hmmmm. Let's talk to them," suggested Willy.

Willy and Margaret met with the maintenance supervisor and asked to see his supply of RJ-45 connectors and crimping tool. "Do you recollect what you paid for this crimping tool?" Willy asked.

"Yeah," the supervisor replied, "$40—it was the best deal I could find."

Willy sighed. "I think it was the worst deal you ever made. Good crimping tools cost well over $100. This tool doesn't let you position the plug properly, and you'd need a grip of iron to exert enough force to get good compression on the connector. Look here, these jaws bend out of alignment when you squeeze the handle." Willy didn't want to sound critical, but settling for cheap tools was one of his pet peeves. Then he examined the supply of RJ-45 plugs in the box with the crimping tool.

"Oh-oh," he said. "These connectors are for solid wire, but you've got stranded wire in your station cables. See here, these connectors only have two prongs per wire, and these prongs are supposed to trap and hold the solid wire. After a while, the stranded wire squishes away from the prongs. It happens whether you touch the station cable or not, but it happens faster when the cable gets yanked and moved during cleaning and other daily activities. Connectors for stranded wire have a single, wide serrated conductor that grabs and traps the wire strands, but they won't work on solid wire."

"So the connectors we have on every cable going to every PC are little time bombs waiting to go off," Margaret said. "Willy, can I get OK Cable to replace them all?"

Willy was already flipping open his case and reaching for the industrial-grade crimping tool that would be more than adequate for the job.

Like a chain, a network cabling system is only as strong as its weakest link. The weakest link in a cabling system is often the station cable, which runs from the wall to the desktop. A first-class cabling installation deserves high-quality connectors. Otherwise, that excellent system will perform as badly as a third-class system—or worse.

In a structured cabling system, the link between the wiring closet and the network node is typically unshielded twisted-pair wire, although it can also be fiber-optic cable. This configuration, and the physically similar IBM Wiring Plan, lends itself to using information outlets, connectors, and separate cables between the wall plates and the network nodes. Even if you use a thin Ethernet system with coaxial cable running from node to node, a wall plate adds reliability and security, but an information outlet and the associated cable connectors can also be a source of electrical noise, high resistance, and crosstalk. Exercise care to ensure that you retain the quality of your installation.

The three pieces of the final link that are most frequent sources of serious problems are the connector on the information outlet, the connectors on the station cable, and the station cable itself. Because people move and change their desks and equipment, that cable and those connectors are subject to more wear and tear than any other portion of the network. This abuse makes them quite prone to failure. In addition, the connection between copper wires and a metal connector must comply with strict installation steps; if it doesn't, the weakest link will be doubly fragile. This chapter addresses the three pieces of the final link in the network, and suggests strategies for avoiding trouble.

■ Information Outlets

You'll typically use wall plates as the point of connection between the horizontal wiring and the station cable extending to the node. But wall plates are just one alternative among various "information outlets." These products include so-called "monument" outlets that stick up from the floor, outlets buried in the floor, and even outlets that pop up out of desktops.

Information outlets are a two-edged sword. On the one hand, you need them because they protect the horizontal wiring from the physical handling that cables receive when employees clean around desks and move computer equipment. They also keep the installation neat and eliminate the unsightly snake pit of unused cables coiled on the floor. However, information outlets introduce two additional connectors (one on the outlet and one on the mating station cable) to a cable that would otherwise run unbroken from the wiring closet to the node or from node to node, and every connector is a potential source of network problems. You need information outlets, but they *must* be carefully installed.

The latest buzzword in information outlets is "modular." Several companies, including Amp and Mod-Tap, sell outlets that can hold a variety of connectors ranging from the common RJ-45 to more exotic token-ring and fiberoptic attachments. You can also find modules with coaxial BNC connectors (see "The BNC Coaxial Connector" later for more details). These modular units snap in and out of the outlet frame, so you can configure and modify outlets to meet your organization's needs. When you use a modular connector, it doesn't matter if you use unshielded twisted-pair, shielded twisted-pair, or coaxial cable in your wiring scheme, and it doesn't matter if the cable is in a star configuration or a daisy-chain; there is an information outlet for you.

The connection at the back side of the information outlet (the side toward the wiring closet in a star-wired system) has an easy life because it typically isn't subject to movement or strain. Connecting unshielded twisted-pair wire to modular RJ-45 jacks is the simplest process—another plus for UTP. With a typical modular jack, the wires press into slots in the back of the jack, as shown in Figure 8.1. A slotted plastic "keeper" snaps over the slots to hold the wires firmly in place. Metal fingers in the slots pierce the insulation of the wires to make the electrical connection. There is no wire stripping and very little untwisting required to make the connection.

Figure 8.1

This Mod-Tap system makes it easy to attach unshielded twisted-pair cable to two RJ-45 jacks. The ends of the module are color-coded to indicate which wire pair matches each pair of connections.

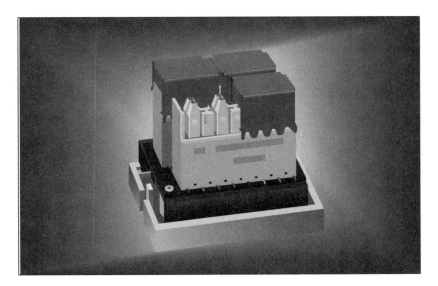

TIP. *Whenever you use UTP or STP, keep the wire twisted just as much as it was originally. Untwist the smallest amount possible when making a connection. The twisting shields against crosstalk, so don't sacrifice even an inch of that protection!*

Information outlet connections on the back side of shielded twisted-pair and coaxial cable modular connectors are practically identical to the connections for the station cable.

■ The Station Cable

The station cable, sometimes confusingly called patch cable (a term that should be reserved for patch cables used in wiring closets), runs between the information outlet and the network node, that is, between the wall and the desktop. Station cables, with the exception of thin Ethernet, use stranded wire to improve the flexibility of the cable and its resistance to breaks caused by metal fatigue.

While you might think of the station cable as a simple piece of wire, some configurations make it an active part of the network. For example, many companies sell cables specially configured with "media filters" that allow you to connect a token-ring network interface card designed for shielded twisted-pair cable to unshielded twisted-pair horizontal wiring. Figure 8.2 shows a cable equipped with a media filter. You can also buy cables equipped with devices called *baluns* that allow you to connect thin Ethernet (10Base2) network interface cards designed for coaxial cable to a UTP system. These specialized station cables let you use the network interface cards you already own even when you install a new structured wiring system.

Figure 8.2

A station cable equipped with a media filter connects a network interface card and an unshielded twisted-pair horizontal wiring system. With this type of cable, you can continue to use your old interface cards even with a new wiring system.

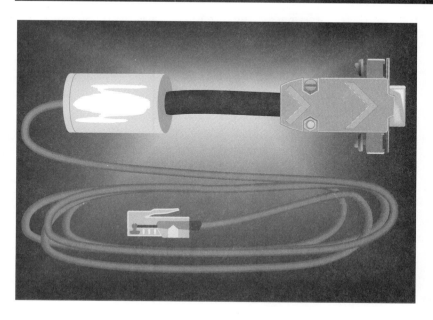

The connectors on the station cable are often a point of failure in network systems, so they deserve special attention.

Cable Connectors

We'll focus on three types of cable connectors in this chapter: RJ-45, BNC, and token-ring data connectors. RJ-45 connectors are used in Ethernet, token-ring, and ARCnet installations. BNC connectors are small coaxial cable connectors used in thin Ethernet and ARCnet. However, Ethernet and ARCnet cables each have a different outside diameter; the connectors and tools are also slightly different. Token-ring data connectors, despite their imposing appearance, are actually the easiest to install properly.

The RJ-45 Connector

The 8-wire RJ-45 connector is the joy of UTP cabling systems. The positive click of an RJ-45 practically guarantees a good connection between the plug and the socket. This connector is small, inexpensive, and, if you have the right tools, easy to install.

When is an RJ-45 connector not an RJ-45 connector? When it's a WEW8. Actually, a WEW8 and an RJ-45 are the same thing. Similarly, the smaller six-wire RJ-11 connector is a WEW6, but the naming schemes originated with different companies. The WE designations were part of the old Western Electric nomenclature, but they are still used in the industry.

NOTE. *The common use of the terms* RJ-45 *and* RJ-11 *is not strictly correct. The device we call an RJ-45 is technicaly an eight-position plug or jack, and the RJ-11 is a six-position plug or jack. The letters "RJ" stand for registered jack and are supposed to connote a specific wiring sequence. We would prefer not to perpetuate this incorrect usage, but if you ask a supplier or installer for an eight-position jack, you'll probably get a blank stare, while everyone undertands RJ-45.*

Telephone wiring people use the term *polarization* to describe the physical form and configuration of the connectors, and you'll often hear the phrase "polarization and sequence." Sequence refers to the order of the wire pairs in the connectors, so taken together, these terms describe the connectors and how they attach to the cable.

Both RJ-45 and BNC connectors depend on force, typically applied by a crimping tool, to make a secure mechanical connection. An RJ-45 crimping tool, shown in Figure 8.3, is often called a plug presser because of its pressing action. When you connect the plug to the cable, you place a plastic connector in a die in the jaw of the crimping tool, carefully dress and insert the wires into the open connector, and then close the handles of the crimping tool to force the connector together.

Because of the force required, the crimping tool must have a sturdy frame and broad handles. A good crimping tool will more than pay for itself, while a cheap one will only lead to headaches—and lots of them. Companies like Amp, General Machine Products, and Mod-Tap make excellent tools. The Mod-Tap Modular Crimping Tool has a handy set of wire cutters in the handle that make the whole job fast and easy.

Figure 8.3

A good crimping tool is invaluable when you make RJ-45 connections. This Mod-Tap Modular Crimping Tool has a sturdy frame, broad handles, a wire stripper, and strong jaws.

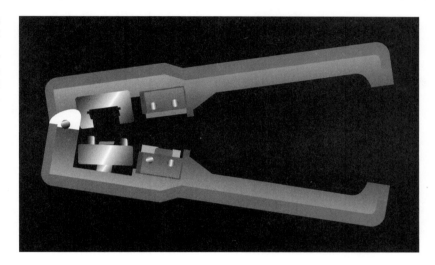

Tip and Ring

If you are involved in cabling, at some time you will hear the terms *tip* and *ring*. These terms harken back to the earliest days of the telephone industry and refer to each of the two wires that connect to the end of a switchboard telephone plug (the tip) or to the back portion of the plug's connecting surface (the ring). Using the terms tip and ring is like saying the plus wire and the minus wire. So, in modern use, tip and ring designate each wire in a pair. The wires in the first pair in a cable or a connector are designated as T1 and R1, the second pair is T2 and R2, and so on.

In UTP horizontal wiring, there is general agreement on how to color code the wires in a cable. In a four-pair cable, the tip conductors (T1 through T4) in each pair are white with a stripe of a secondary color that designates the pair. The ring conductors (R1 through R4) have jackets of the secondary color with a white stripe.

The secondary colors used in a 4-pair cable are blue, orange, green, and brown. The color slate is also assigned as a secondary color in cables with more wire pairs. So in UTP connections, wire T1 is white with a blue stripe, while its partner R1 is blue with a white stripe. Wire T2 is white with an orange stripe, and R2 is orange with a white stripe, and so on. Some cables, like those connecting the 50-pin telco connectors used in wiring closets, need more pairs, so red, black, yellow, and violet are assigned as other primary colors. Used together, the five primary and five secondary colors identify all pairs in a 25-pair cable.

If only the rest were so simple. It would seem that it should be easy to agree on which wire pairs connect to which pins on a plug. Unfortunately, there isn't one set of agreements but rather at least eight agreed-upon (by various companies and associations) sequences for mating UTP wires and connectors. Here is a short list and description.

USOC. The Universal Service Order Code (USOC) is the oldest specification. It is derived from original Bell System specifications, so it is widely used by telephone companies. Note that the USOC system arranges the pair sequences from the center out. Specifically notice that pins 1 and 2 are not a part of the same pair as they are in the other common configurations. The USOC wiring pattern doesn't conform to the 10Base-T network specifications, but then a USOC-wired installation probably doesn't meet the data service requirements for crosstalk or noise either. **Caution:** Don't use USOC for data.

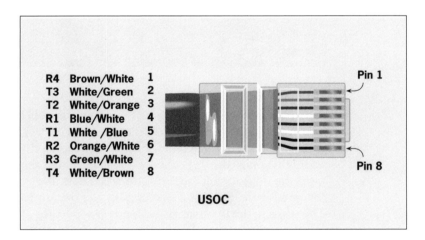

R4	Brown/White	1
T3	White/Green	2
T2	White/Orange	3
R1	Blue/White	4
T1	White /Blue	5
R2	Orange/White	6
R3	Green/White	7
T4	White/Brown	8

Pin 1

Pin 8

USOC

EIA Preferred Commercial Building Specification. Despite its imposing title, this isn't the sequence we prefer. However, you won't go wrong using this sequence, as long as everyone who works on the cabling knows that your building is "EIA-standard."

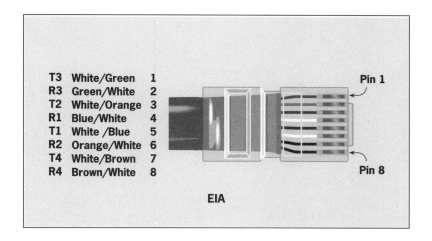

T3	White/Green	1
R3	Green/White	2
T2	White/Orange	3
R1	Blue/White	4
T1	White /Blue	5
R2	Orange/White	6
T4	White/Brown	7
R4	Brown/White	8

EIA

AT&T 258A. This is the configuration we recommend and the one used by most installers. Pairs T2/R2 and T3/R3 carry the data. You should never simultaneously use pairs T1/R1 or T4/R4 for voice; instead, use those pairs for spares or for future high-speed data requirements that might demand more than two pairs. In some installations, pins 7 and 8 are left open; this configuration is designated as AT&T 356A.

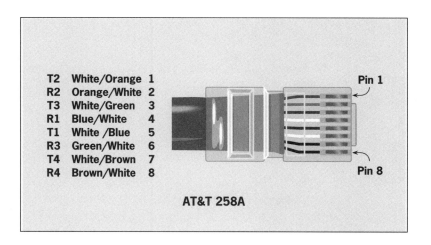

T2	White/Orange	1
R2	Orange/White	2
T3	White/Green	3
R1	Blue/White	4
T1	White /Blue	5
R3	Green/White	6
T4	White/Brown	7
R4	Brown/White	8

AT&T 258A

IEEE 10Base-T. The IEEE simply took the AT&T standard and stripped out the pairs normally used for voice. We think you will find the R1/T1 pair useful as a spare.

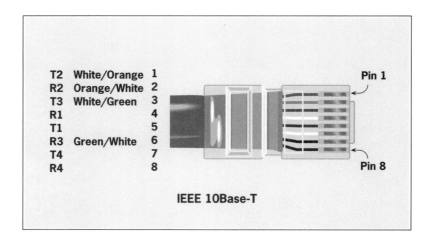

T2 White/Orange 1
R2 Orange/White 2
T3 White/Green   3
R1   4
T1   5
R3 Green/White   6
T4   7
R4   8

Pin 1
Pin 8

IEEE 10Base-T

Rolm and Digital. Not only do Rolm and Digital Equipment Corporation have their own wiring sequences, but Digital also sometimes uses different plugs and jacks. Older Digital Equipment installations use a particularly obnoxious proprietary plug (the modified modular plug or MMJ) that has its little, plastic, locking tab offset to the side instead of in the center.

The fundamental connection concepts for the Digital and Rolm systems are exactly the same as the other sequence schemes, and Digital's Open DECconnect is compatible with AT&T 258A and the 10Base-T specification, except that Digital leaves T4/R4 as a spare and keeps T1/R1 (pins 4 and 5) open.

While the wiring and color-coding scheme described above works for horizontal cables, patch cables have their own color-coding scheme. The wires inside the patch cables use solid colors in the following sequence:

T1 Green

R1 Red

T2 Black

R2 Yellow

T3 Blue

R3 Orange

T4 Brown

R4 White

HINT. *Some telephone systems use patch cables that reverse the sequence of the wires from end to end. Patch cables designed for data applications have the connectors on each end wired in the same sequence. Keep reversed patch cables away from your data patch panels.*

If you're using RJ-45 connectors in your system, we suggest that you keep in mind the following considerations:

- Carefully count the number of RJ-45 connectors you think you'll need, and then add 50 percent more to the order. Your needs will grow faster than you can imagine.

- If you ever put the wires in the wrong order or suspect that one wire isn't properly seated in the RJ-45 connector, cut the connector off and start over. Don't try to open or reseal the connector because it will fail to work correctly in the long run.

- Different connectors are sold for stranded wire and for solid wire. Be sure to use the appropriate connectors in every case.

- Carefully match the tip and ring pairs. Improperly connecting the wires in a pair so that they are not part of the same circuit (a condition called *split pairs*) is the major source of twisted-pair wiring problems.

The BNC Coaxial Connector

BNC connectors make a neat looking connection, and the male connectors lock on to the female connectors with a reassuring snap. Despite this small comfort, BNC connectors can have hidden, intermittent short circuits that frustrate attempts at troubleshooting because they disappear when you touch them.

You can buy several types of BNC connectors, but we strongly suggest avoiding the so-called "crimpless" connectors. Crimpless connectors use screw-on sections to hold the pieces together, and in our hard-won experience, they are not as reliable as a connector with a good crimp.

The previously proffered advice about buying a good quality crimping tool is triply important with BNC connectors. The handle and jaws of the tool should ratchet—you should be able to give it one squeeze to get it tight and then another good squeeze to really make the crimp. The jaws of the tool should be wide enough to cover the entire crimped sleeve at one time. When you use a tool with a narrow jaw, you'll have to make several crimps on the sleeve, they won't be uniform, and the cable can eventually flow out from the crimps. Anything less than a tool with a wide and strong ratcheting jaw is simply unacceptable.

Figure 8.4 shows the correct dimensions of a piece of cable stripped and prepared for a BNC connector. Careful preparation of the cable is critical to making a connection that doesn't short between the tip and the ring of the connector or that doesn't have an open circuit between the ring of the connector and the copper braid of the cable.

Figure 8.4

There are two keys to making a good BNC connection: proper preparation of the cable and a good crimp. Many crimping tools have a life-size diagram on the stripped cable on the handle. Follow the dimensions carefully.

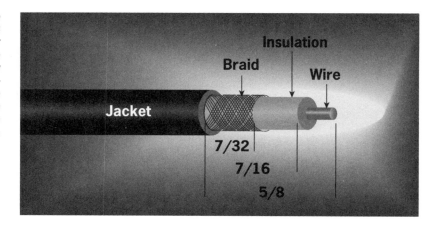

The assembly sequence for every connector is usually shown on the packaging for the connector. Don't forget to crimp the silver or gold tip before you insert it into the body of the connector.

Dress the braid carefully so it is completely under, but not over, the crimp-down collar. A good, professionally installed connector, shown in Figure 8.5, might have just a hint of braid showing between the shoulder of the crimp.

Figure 8.5

A good crimp on the sleeve of the BNC connector is critical to a good connection. The jaws of the crimping tool should span most of the sleeve, and copper braid should not be dressed back over the sleeve.

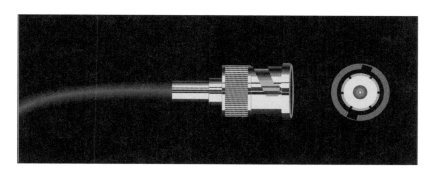

The Token-Ring Data Connector

What is ugly, expensive, and easy to use? A token-ring data connector. Although there are fancy tools available, you really only need a knife or wire stripper and a pair of pliars to install a token-ring data connector on the end of a shielded twisted-pair cable.

The process is easier to do than to read about. Refer to Figure 8.6 and follow these steps:

Figure 8.6

The token-ring connector literally snaps together. With the shielding removed, the wires fit into special barrel connectors, and a plastic keeper forces the wires into slots that cut the insulation and make the connection.

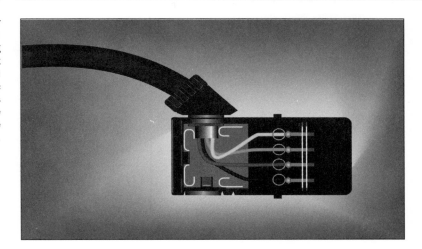

1. Strip $1\frac{1}{8}$ inches of the outer jacket off the cable.

2. Cut off 1 inch of the copper braid and the same amount of the foil surrounding each pair.

3. Fit the cable through the threaded sleeve of the connector.

4. Fold the braid against the connector's metal frame.

5. Slide each wire into its own connection barrel connector.

6. Put the plastic retainer on top of the posts, and squeeze it down with the pliers. A special tool is available to do this, but we don't think you'll need one. The post pierces the insulation and makes a positive electrical contact. The plastic post even shows you the correct wire sequence: red, green, orange, black. The red and green wires are the first pair, and the orange and black wires are the second pair.

7. Snap the cover on the open side of the plug and you're done.

Wall plates for data connectors follow the same process. It is important but not difficult to ensure that the braid makes solid contact with the metal interior of the plug. From the point of view of the installer, the data connectors are the best thing about the IBM cable plan.

Connectors are *so* important. Take the time and make the investment to install them properly.

- *Light through the Tunnel*
- *Signaling and Connection Standards*

9

Fiber-optic Cable

Willy had mixed feelings about thunderstorms. The destructive tornadoes they often spawned were terrifying, but the lightning strikes were good for business. The morning after a thunderstorm, he would receive plenty of cries for help— particularly from organizations with multiple buildings connected by copper cables. Early this morning, a thunderstorm had crossed the city, and about an hour after the spectacular lightning departed, the phone began ringing. He had already dispatched three crews on emergency calls and was trying to reschedule the day's new installations and routine maintenance when the phone rang again.

"Hi, I'm calling from the Broadview Country Club and we have a problem with our computers." Willy could hear the problem in the background. The exclusive country club was 30 miles out of town, and apparently the caller was right under the traveling lightning storm. The circuit crackled as thunder boomed.

"Get off the phone and I'll be out there in time for lunch," Willy promptly replied.

Over lunch with the club manager, Willy learned that the country club's far-flung pro shop, restaurant and pool, and maintenance facilities were connected by a mile of buried multipair cable that was used for both voice and data. Devices called line drivers—similar to high-powered modems—were used to move data over the cable. Every time there was a lightning storm in the area, one or more line drivers "popped," the club manager's word for what Willy saw as a smoking ruin of wires and plastic.

"You'll have this problem until you lay fiber-optic cables," Willy explained. "For you, the most important benefit of fiber is the complete freedom from worry about lightning or other electrical problems. But you'll also benefit from higher speeds between the three facilities. You should get rid of those 9,600-bit per-second line drivers, use wiring hubs with ports for both the fiber and for regular copper unshielded twisted-pair wire, and have a high-speed network that covers the whole club."

Willy walked the manager through the details of the installation. In some areas, the club already had a buried conduit, and Willy's crew could use a commercial vacuum cleaner to suck a string, taped to a little plastic ball, through the conduit. Using the string, his crew would pull through the only slightly larger dual fiber. In other places, including a run across a fairway, the fiber would have to be directly buried, but Willy explained that this would require only a small slit, not a wide trench. The club would need three new wiring hubs with fiber ports to use the new cables. Willy promised to fax a proposal the next day.

As Willy walked toward his truck, he noticed how unusually green the grass was and how healthy the trees looked. "Yes," he thought, "a little lightning can sometimes do some good."

Fiber-optic cable is wonderful stuff. It offers freedom from electrical grounding and lightning problems, and transmission speeds in the range of hundreds of megabits per second. Because it is free of crosstalk and interference from outside noise sources, you can use it to connect over much longer distances than is possible with copper cables. It would certainly replace copper cables for every data application—if it wasn't so expensive.

The rule of thumb is that labor is the most expensive part of any cable installation. The exception to that rule is fiber-optic installations. On a per-foot basis, fiber is about three times as expensive as thin Ethernet coaxial cable and about seven times as expensive as high quality 3- or 4-pair UTP. The cost of the fiber-optic cable itself exceeds the cost of labor in many geographical regions.

On a per-connection basis, fiber-optic cable connectors are less expensive than the IBM data connectors used on STP in IBM Token-Ring installations, but hundreds of times more expensive than RJ-45 connectors. However, the real cost of fiber lies in the training, practice, and tools needed to make a good fiber-optic connection.

On the bottom line, our best advice is to use fiber-optic cables where they make the most sense, particularly between buildings and often between wiring closets within buildings. Only organizations in very special situations, perhaps those with long cable runs or those operating in electrically noisy or explosive environments, can cost-justify running fiber-optic cable to desktops.

When you need to add fiber to your installation, you can either hire an outside contractor with a proven track record or send some of your own people to school to learn how to install connectors. Without the proper training and tools, installing fiber is not a do-it-yourself project.

■ Light through the Tunnel

A piece of commercial fiber-optic cable contains two pipes for light. Each pipe, or glass strand, carries light in one direction, so a cable for digital communications requires two separate strands in the cable. A light source, typically a laser at one end of each glass strand, generates a beam of light that is turned off and on very quickly. These light pulses represent the zeros and ones of a digital signal. A receiver at the end of the cable opposite the light source decodes the signals.

Fiber-optic cable is so effective because the light is tightly contained inside the fiber. Light can't get in or out, so unlike electrical pulses in copper cables, the light pulses are completely isolated from the outside environment. You can run fiber with impunity next to high voltage power lines, radio transmitters, welding machines, and in other environments that would disrupt signals in copper cables.

DANGER! *Never look into the end of a fiber when optical power is applied. The infrared light used in fiber-optic systems is invisible, but it can cause serious injury to the eye. You'll want to look, but don't do it!*

The center of each glass strand, called the *core*, is the conduit for the light. Light from a diode or laser enters the core at one end and is trapped by the shiny walls of the core—a phenomenon called *total internal reflection*. The core is surrounded by a glass or plastic coating, called the *cladding*, that has a different optical density than the core. The boundary between the cladding and the core reflects the light back into the core.

Single-Mode and Multimode

This discussion could quickly become overly complex, so we are going to avoid wading in very far and instead tell you what you need to know to be safe. In commercial use, you'll find two categories of fiber cables: single-mode and multimode. These categories are defined by how light moves inside the cable—that's the aspect we are going to avoid. If you want to delve into the physics and the math, we suggest reading *A Technician's Guide to Fiber Optics*, written by Donald J. Sterling, Jr., and published by Delmar Publishers. Amp and other cable companies may make this book available to commercial installers.

The practical difference between these types of fibers is that single-mode fiber will carry signals farther and faster than multimode, but it is more expensive to buy and more difficult to install. The single-mode fiber is also thinner than the multimode fiber, which makes it even more difficult to work with. In commercial use, single-mode fiber is typically installed in very long distance runs. If you aren't thinking in terms of tens of miles, then you can and should use multimode cable. If you do need to cover these types of distances, then check with your local telephone or cable television companies to subcontract for an experienced installation team.

Multimode fiber-optic cable is commonly used in LANs and campus-wide installations. You will find that multimode cable is available in catalogs in two different core sizes: 62.5 microns and 100 microns. The 100 micron material is now used only in a few instances such as in IBM Token-Ring installations, while the 62.5 micron material is the most widely used. With the smaller core size, the physical size of the fiber itself is about 0.002 inches, and the cladding typically is 125 or 140 microns thick—about 0.003 inches. So the fiber you'll probably use will be listed in the catalog as multimode, graded-index, optical-fiber waveguide with a nominal 62.5/125 micron core/cladding diameter.

Ordering Options

When you order fiber, you face other practical considerations. The same factors that apply to copper cable concerning the fire rating of the cable jacket also apply to fiber-optic cable. Always use plenum-rated cable if you can foresee that it might be needed. Fiber-optic cable products come in versions with reinforced jackets designed for direct burial, and in multifiber versions. Unlike UTP, there are no operational drawbacks to including multiple fibers within the same outer jacket. If you go to the expense of installing fiber between buildings, it makes sense to buy cables that contain more fibers than you have immediate use for to meet future requirements.

Connectors

No book can teach you how to attach fiber-optic connectors. Amp, Mod-Tap, and other companies offer formal courses, typically one or two days long, in which you can learn the skill. The courses cover methods of "cleaving" (cutting) the cable and various polishing techniques to reduce loss of light through the "window" at the end of the cable. Most of the class time is devoted to hands-on practice, so there is a relatively high cost for class materials.

All fiber-optic connectors attempt to transmit light in the most efficient manner. To do so, the ends of the fibers must be cleaved at a perfect right angle, polished thoroughly to remove scratches, and then attached so the plug and jack meet in perfect alignment. That is tricky and painstaking work requiring physical dexterity and patience.

If you hire an outside contractor, you'll want an installer who is quite experienced putting connectors on fiber cables. Let them learn and practice on someone else's time; you should buy experience. If you are training your own installers, provide them with incentives to stay with your company after the training and be prepared to pay well over $1,000 for the equipment needed by each trainee. In addition, investing several thousand dollars more in devices such as curing ovens and inspection microscopes can speed the work of an installation team.

There are at least eight types of fiber-optic connectors in common use, but practically, you only need to know about four: the ST, SMA, MIC, and SC.

The ST connector, shown in an exploded view in Figure 9.1, is the most commonly used connector in commercial installations. Originally designed by AT&T, it has been adopted by many companies. Most courses teach the techniques of installing ST connectors.

Figure 9.1

The ST connector only has a few parts, but the installer must carefully cleave the fiber at a right angle, position the fiber for maximum signal transfer, and polish the end of the fiber to remove scratches that would degrade the signal.

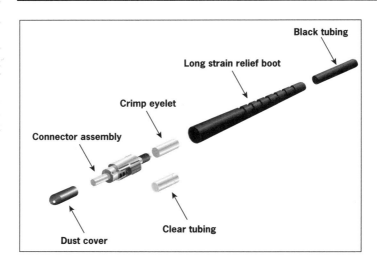

The center of the ST connector is a ceramic sleeve or ferrule, 2.5 mm in size, that is glued to the fiber. The fiber itself appears at the end of the ferrule. To transmit the greatest amount of light, it must be polished by hand or by machine until it is free of scratches. The outer shell of the ST connector is similar to the shell of the BNC coaxial connector in that the plug locks on to the jack with a quarter twist. ST connectors work well in commercial and office environments.

Some equipment, particularly equipment from European manufacturers, uses a connector called the SMA that looks similar to the ST but uses a threaded outer shell. This type of connection is more rugged, particularly under the stress of vibrations. The SMA connector, developed by Amp, has been standardized by NATO and the United States military. There are two styles of the SMA connector, one with a blunt tip like the ST connector and another with a stepped-down tip for better alignment. If you have equipment that uses these connectors, make sure your installer knows exactly which style of SMA plug is required.

As we explained earlier, fiber-optic cables use two fiber strands, each of which carries light in one direction. The two strands are connected together in a manner that makes the fiber-optic cable look something like the power cord for a lamp. The ST and SMA connector systems use a single connector on each strand. Although the outer jacket of one fiber in each pair carries a stripe or other specific marking, most problems during installations, moves, and changes result from the wrong fiber being plugged into the wrong jack.

The Medium Interface Connector (MIC), adopted by the American National Standards Institute as a part of the Fiber Distributed Data Interface (FDDI) architecture, eliminates that problem. Unlike the ST and SMA connectors, a single MIC connector, shown in Figure 9.2, holds two fibers and is keyed so the plug and socket can only attach one way. MIC connectors are used in many brands of wiring hubs and LAN adapters, in addition to FDDI systems.

Figure 9.2

The MIC connector, typically associated with FDDI, holds two fibers and is keyed to insure proper polarity between the male and female plugs.

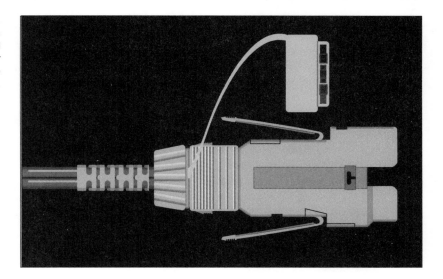

In some applications, you might find a connector called the SC style connector. The SC connector provides a very strong "pull proof" connection that is sometimes used in cable splices. Like the SMA, the SC connector can handle two fibers and ensures that they connect properly. It is, however, a difficult connector to install. Our best advice is to always avoid splices.

There is one significant drawback to the dual-cable connection scheme in the MIC and SC connectors: If the installer makes one good connection but then makes a bad cut or does a sloppy job of gluing the second connection, the good connection is wasted because the installer must cut off both connections to start over again. This drawback explains the popularity of the single ST and SMA connectors and drives the need for particularly experienced and careful installers if you use MIC or SC connectors.

While it is very likely that new equipment you order will be equipped with ST connectors, it always pays to check. You can intermix equipment with other connectors in an installation—the connectors at one end of the cable don't dictate what connectors must be at the other end of the cable—but your installer must know what to expect. The MIC connectors are growing in popularity, and you should consider using them, particularly if the installer quotes a flat rate for the job.

■ Signaling and Connection Standards

You should be familiar with three standards for signaling over fiber and for making fiber-optic cable connections: FDDI, the fiber-optic inter repeater link (FOIRL), and the 10Base-F standard that is part of the IEEE 802.3 (Ethernet) specifications. Primarily, you must know about these standards to make sure you order equipment that can work together. Beyond that, the operation of the equipment conforming to these standards is invisible to you.

FDDI

FDDI is complex. The full specification includes two rings of fiber-optic cable that send frames of data in opposite directions. If one cable is broken in the primary ring, data completes its trip in the secondary ring. FDDI equipment is highly reliable and fast, using 100 megabit-per-second signaling. But few people need all of the features of FDDI, and we predict that it will be bypassed in the rush of technology toward other schemes such as Asynchronous Transfer Mode—an emerging technology for fast signaling that can use high-grade UTP cable plants. Due to this and other stresses, the original concept of FDDI is changing rapidly.

Even the word "fiber" in the acronym FDDI is misleading. Under the latest definition of the American National Standards Institute, the term FDDI can include fiber-optic, shielded twisted-pair, or unshielded twisted-pair cable—so the term FDDI no longer necessarily implies fiber.

FDDI is a networking scheme that gains high reliability through redundancy and sophisticated data handling protocols. The fiber-optic cable alternative in FDDI provides signaling out to 2 kilometers, but the higher costs of fiber have limited its popularity. The FDDI protocols can run over copper cable to a maximum distance of 100 meters and require a Level 5 UTP installation.

An ANSI committee has approved a plan for signaling using two pairs of Level 5 UTP. This plan uses a transmission scheme called Multi-Level Transmission-3 (MLT-3), which randomizes data to reduce emissions, and also specifies a method of equalizing signal levels.

At the same time, IBM and other vendors are pushing for the use of FDDI protocols over shielded twisted-pair wire, a proposal that goes by the name SDDI. IBM, Network Peripherals, and SynOptics are among the companies shipping SDDI modules for their chassis-based wiring hubs.

Crescendo Communications uses the term Copper Distributed Data Interface (CDDI) to describe its products that use the FDDI techniques over unshielded twisted-pair. Other companies like Network Peripherals use the term FDDI over UTP to describe their products that conform to the ANSI draft standard.

At this point, neither CDDI nor SDDI can prioritize time-sensitive data like full-motion video. Another ANSI committee is working on FDDI II, a new architecture that adds a priority capability for time-sensitive packets.

ANSI is developing a standard called Low Cost Fiber (LCF) that offers cost reductions and requires less skill to install. The LCF fiber itself doesn't cost any less—in fact, the cable is the same—but the specifications for the transceivers and connectors have been loosened. In turn, the maximum distance has been reduced to 1 kilometer, but that isn't a limiting factor in most installations. The LCF reduces the cost of a fiber-optic installation by 25 to 35 percent.

FOIRL and 10Base-F

While FDDI took advantage of the quality of the signal traveling over a fiber-optic link to increase the signaling speed to 100 megabits per second, other standards are content (for now at least) to only extend the distance or operational capability.

The fiber-optic interrepeater link (FOIRL) specification was created to describe how Ethernet repeaters should communicate over fiber-optic cable. The goal of the FOIRL design is to integrate fiber into certain critical points in an Ethernet network in order to extend the distance of operation or to allow operation in environments with high levels of electrical noise.

FOIRL is an old specification, but many transceivers (external devices that connect to the AUI port on an Ethernet adapter) follow the FOIRL standard. The FOIRL standard allows connection of repeaters over at least 2 km of cable. FOIRL devices typically use ST connectors.

The only trick to employing FOIRL is making sure you have compatible devices on both ends of the link. Wiring hubs might have FOIRL ports to link to other hubs, but the connections to the desktop LAN adapters typically use a different scheme. FOIRL is designed to extend copper cable, not to replace it.

The strategy for replacing copper cable with fiber cable is described in a newer standard called 10Base-F. This standard, which includes two variations called 10Base-FB and 10Base-FL, are products of the same IEEE committee process that delivered 10Base-T. 10Base-FL describes the connections between LAN nodes and a cable hub, while 10Base-FB describes a backbone connection between cable hubs. The difference between the two lies in the signaling, and both standards allow for cable runs of up to 2 kilometers.

While products conforming to these standards typically stay with Ethernet's 10 megabit-per-second signaling, there is no technical reason for this limitation. The Ethernet standard can easily support signaling speeds of 100 megabits per second and faster, and these standards will certainly evolve in this direction.

It is relatively easy to order LAN adapters and wiring hubs that have 10Base-FB or 10Base-FL ports. Typically, you'll mix in as much fiber as you need to extend the network or to carry the network into areas of high electrical noise while still relying on less expensive copper adapters in other parts of the network.

Practical Installations

Overall, the use of multimode fiber-optic cable can be just as simple as we've presented it here—order the right equipment and connectors, keep distances down to 2 kilometers or less, and they should work together. Longer installations require the use of calculators to work out "power budgets" (the amount of light that must enter the cable to be detectable at the receiver) and other factors, so we suggest leaving them to experienced professionals.

Here are a few hints gained from experience:

- Order related products from the same manufacturer. If you can, buy your LAN adapters and cable hubs from the same company, purchase your cables and connectors from the same company, and get your connectors and tools from the same company. Things just work better than way.

- Because fiber-optic cable is so small and flexible, it's easy to forget that there is a piece of glass inside. Be particularly careful of the bend radius of the cable when it goes around walls and in other tight places. As a practical rule, never bend a cable in a circle with a radius of less than 2 inches and, if there is any force on the cable, keep the bend radius to 6 inches or more.

- Because fiber-optic cable is small and flexible, it's easy to snake it into conduits with other cables. Electrically, this isn't a problem, but the weight of heavy copper cables can crush the cladding on the fiber-optic cable and cause the cable to leak light. Keep heavy weights off the fiber.

- Even small bends, so called *microbends,* can cause light to leak into the jacket. Avoid using a great deal of force to pull a fiber, because it might cause a microbend that will ruin a section of cable.

- Avoid splicing cable whenever possible. New cable installations should never use spliced cables. If a cable must be spliced to restore service, the installer should choose an appropriate splice kit from any of several on the market. The type of splice kit is not driven by the type of connectors used on the ends of the cable. Cleaving, gluing, and polishing the ends of the cable in the splice kit while working inside a wall is no fun.

- Use fiber to extend copper cable networks where it makes sense. A good UTP cable installation can carry a lot of data and is less costly, so use both UTP and fiber cables to their best advantage.

- *What Cable Testers Measure*
- *Testing Fiber*
- *Baseline and Certification*

10

Cable Testing and Certification

"This room wasn't here before! It's not on our plans," exclaimed Willy, looking over the top of the plans he was holding and fixing the network manager with a glare. "What did you do with the cables that were in this space when you built the room?" he asked.

"We put them in the false ceiling. We didn't disconnect anything, so they should be OK," the manager replied. Willy stopped himself from adding, Then why am I here? The client had a problem and he was here to fix it even if the problem resulted from the client's careless actions.

Willy got a short ladder from his truck, removed a ceiling tile, and poked his head into the false ceiling space. The high-quality Level 5 cables coming from the wiring closet were there, but instead of laying in the hangers his crew had installed, they were bent sharply around metal ceiling brackets, stretched directly over the new fluorescent lights, and crisscrossed over AC power cables at every angle.

"Look," Willy explained, "the connectors are important, but it's what happens to the cables in between the connections that counts. We'll have to do a new profile on each wire pair in each cable your people moved—then we'll know what we've got."

The network manager seemed interested, so Willy explained the process as he removed a device about the size of a paperback James Michener novel from its case. He unpacked a small printer, connected the two with a cable, and then moved the whole system to a wall jack. "This is a Microtest Penta Scanner. We'll take it from jack to jack, where it will scan each wire pair, check the level of electrical noise in several frequency bands, measure crosstalk between pairs, and compare the results to the published standards."

Then he removed a thick printout from his soft-sided satchel and thumped it down on a desk. "We'll compare this profile from the initial installation with the results we get today, and then we'll know what we need to do."

Willy used a low-power walkie-talkie to coordinate with an assistant standing at the patch panel in the wiring closet. The assistant moved the Penta Scanner's signal source from cable to cable so the scanner could measure against a known signal. It took longer for the printer to produce each report than it did for the Microtest scanner to perform its tests.

A few minutes later Willy had the printouts spread in front of him on the network manager's desk. "Well, across the board these cables have higher levels of low-frequency noise than they had before. That noise comes from the power wiring and lights, but it only exceeds the standard on these two cables. The near-end crosstalk is very high on this cable, so I imagine it has a pretty good kink in it, probably around a metal bracket. Looks like a couple hours of work overall. Without the scanner, we'd have spent the entire day replacing all the cables."

As Willy walked out to the parking lot, he reflected that as a result of investing a few thousand dollars in a modern cable tester, he had a happy customer but a shorter billable day. He hoped this customer's long-term business would make up for the hours he had saved this time. "Oh well," he reflected, "I'd rather be fixing things for real than spinning my wheels in frustration."

Your network can't be better than its cables, but how good are those cables? That's the most important question you can ask during installation and troubleshooting. Even if you use the best quality cable, connectors, patch panels, jumpers, and hubs, sloppy installation or a hostile electrical environment can prevent your network from operating at peak potential. To diagnose the electrical environment that the LAN adapter's signals pass through in the cable, you must test the entire installation in place.

Once a good cable system is installed, what do you do when problems arise? Unfortunately, network cable problems can closely mimic network software problems. If a network cable has high noise or high near-end crosstalk, the networking software might respond by working overtime sending extra frames of data to push the message through. If the software reaches an impasse, it can generate an error message like NetWare's familiar "Server Not Found." Dozens of types of problems can cause that message to appear, so you must troubleshoot the problem to find the true source.

Whether you're troubleshooting problems with your kitchen toaster or the internal navigation system on a Boeing 747, you follow the same procedure:

- Logically break the system into functional elements.

- Based on the symptoms, determine the most likely dysfunctional element.

- Use testing or substitution to determine if the suspect element is in fact bad.

- If the suspect element is not bad, move to the next likely suspect.

- When, through testing or substitution you find the dysfunctional element, repair or replace it.

Substituting one cable for another to test for a dysfunctional element does not offer certain proof of anything, because a common problem can effect all cables. Your best bet is to compare recorded measurements taken when the system was working properly against current measurements. This amounts to testing against an established baseline, and it's as important in cable testing as in medicine and aerospace.

Several companies, notably Datacom Technologies, John Fluke Manufacturing, and Microtest Corporation, market handheld cable testers with a variety of features including the ability to certify that a cable meets specific IEEE or EIA/TIA standards. These devices can operate across several different cable types, providing various functions for each type of cable. Figure 10.1 shows a Microtest cable scanner.

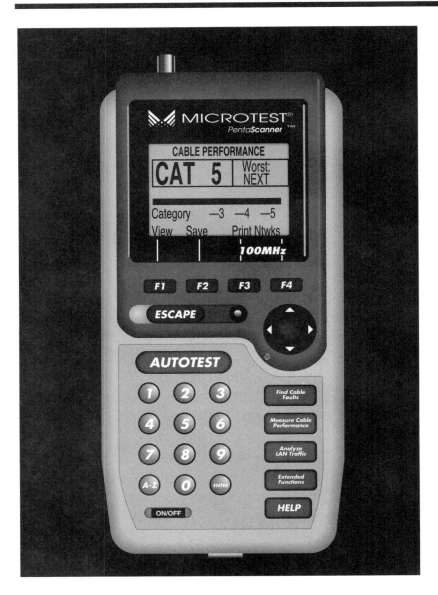

These devices can create either a printout or, when attached to a PC, a data file that you can keep as a baseline for future reference. You can use this record to check a cable's characteristics against a fixed standard and against measurements taken previously. This comparison makes it easy to spot specific problems and to track degradation caused by aging, weather, or other factors. A printout showing the evaluation of a cable against EIA/TIA 568 Level 5 standards is shown in Figure 10.2.

Figure 10.2

This printout compares the test results of a specific cable's attenuation, noise, and near-end crosstalk against the published standards.

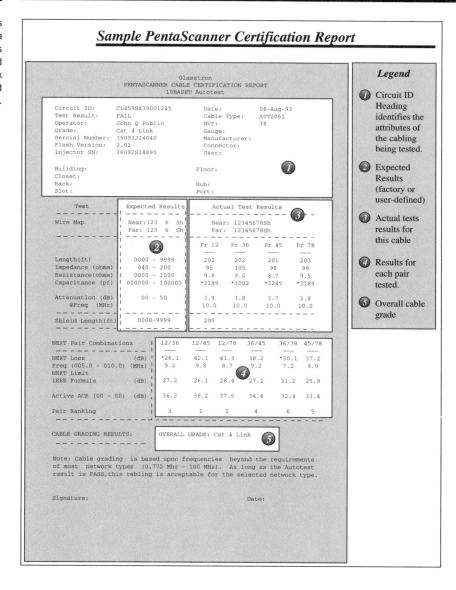

In previous chapters, we told you that installing fiber-optic cable connectors was not a do-it-yourself project and that you need a good electrician to help you with grounding problems. But these handheld cable checkers can be used by any knowledgeable network manager or installer with little or no special training. While they usually come with excellent manuals, the units have simple controls and explanations of their operation that appear on LCD screens. Perhaps the most important tip we can offer regarding these cable scanners is to remember to keep them charged. While they do have external power adapters, these portable cable scanners are much easier to use with full batteries.

■ What Cable Testers Measure

Cable testers come with a variety of capabilities. Since the companies change their models, prices, and features at least every year and a half, we don't try to associate a set of features with a specific product in this book. Instead, we list the features you'll generally find in these devices and let you select the product that meets your needs.

Cable Distance

The various IEEE networking standards specify maximum cable lengths. In the case of IEEE 802.3 (Ethernet), the overall length directly affects the ability of network nodes to share the cable; a cable that is too long degrades the system.

Cable scanners measure the distance to an open-ended or shorted cable by sending a pulse down the cable and then timing its reflection back from the end of the cable, a technique called *time-domain reflectometry* (TDR). Companies like Hewlett-Packard sell very precise and expensive TDR devices for use on long cable runs. The TDR capabilities available in handheld cable checkers is less precise, but good enough for most work. You can expect distance readings to be accurate to about two feet.

When you measure a cable with an electrical pulse instead of a tape measure, the pulse doesn't travel at the same speed in every type of cable. The size of the wires, type of insulation, and external shielding all effect the speed of the electrical pulse. A factor called the *nominal velocity of propagation* (NVP) is the ratio between the speed of an electrical pulse in a specific type of cable and the speed of light. The scanner must apply the appropriate NVP to the cable to accurately measure the cable length. Scanners should contain a table that has the NVP for a variety of cable types, but you also might want to measure the NVP for a particular spool or lot of cable in order to get more accurate distance measurements.

The scanner can calculate the cable's NVP if you know the cable length, so it is wise to carefully measure a few hundred feet of cable from the typical 1,000-foot spool and to use what is usually called the scanner's calibration function to measure the NVP of that known length of cable. Modern cable checkers allow you to enter that figure (typically between 0.6 and 0.9) into a memory for future use.

HINT. *Once you know the NVP of a cable or obtain a standard NVP from the cable checker's memory, it easy to determine how much cable is left on a spool. Put a connector on the cable and use the cable checker to test the cable length; it's a lot easier than unrolling the spool and measuring it foot by foot.*

The distance measurement is particularly useful for finding open or shorted coaxial BNC connectors on thin Ethernet. When a thin Ethernet installation is working properly, you should disconnect every T-connector and take a distance measurement on each cable segment. With all T-connectors disconnected from the cable, you'll see a series of readings on the cable tester like, "Cable open at 30 feet." If you record each of these readings and create a network map, you'll be prepared when a crimped connector shorts out or a T-connector doesn't connect and the network crashes. By retesting the cable and applying a little logic to the changed readings, you'll find the bad connector.

In a UTP installation, taking distance measurements assures you of at least minimal quality on your punch-down blocks or cross-connect panels. When you measure distance on a cable, the cable checker sends a wave that is reflected when it encounters the most distant open connection. If you measure through the punch-down block or cross-connection, you'll know whether the cable check detects a large lump of impedance, like an open circuit. If the cable checker reports the distance to the punch-down block or cross-connect point instead of detecting some more distant point, then you know you have an equipment or connection problem.

Some cable checkers come with a special port for an oscilloscope. If you use a good scope with a 200 MHz bandwidth, you can see the TDR pulse put out by the cable checker, measure its return, and obtain a much finer measurement of cable distance and quality. If you are experienced, the scope trace will show lumped impedances—perhaps marginal connectors—that the cable checker would ignore.

Wire Map

Some cable testers offer a wire map function among the distance measurement features, and others make it a stand-alone function. *Wire map*, a feature unique to twisted-pair installations, shows you which wire pairs connect to what pins on the plugs and sockets. This test quickly detects whether an installer connected the wires to a plug or jack in reverse order—a common problem. It is also valuable for detecting the most common cause of data problems in twisted-pair cabling: split pairs. The split pair condition is shown in Figure 10.3. A similar crossed condition called crossed pairs is also troublesome. You can only spot split pairs through visual inspection or by seeing the effect of a split-pair condition in the crosstalk measurements.

Figure 10.3

The conditions called crossed pair and split pair are similar, but slightly different. A crossed pair reverses the tip and ring. A cable checker that does a wire map will detect this condition. However, split pairs will check out OK on a wire map and can only be detected by checking the near-end crosstalk.

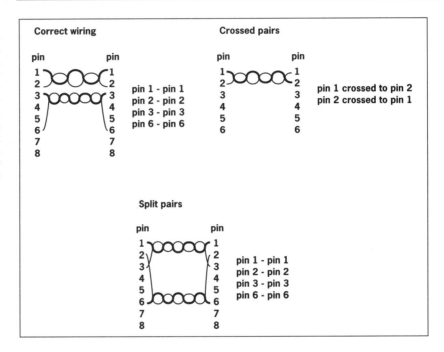

The twisting in wire pairs shields the desirable signals from external signals. This shielding only occurs if the wires in the pair are part of the same circuit. Unfortunately, it's common for the wires in a pair to be accidently split so they are part of different circuits. A current can flow in a circuit and the system appears to work—particularly over short distances and in limited trials—but no self-shielding is protecting the signals, and eventually near-end crosstalk becomes a problem. (Near-end crosstalk is discussed in detail later in this chapter.)

Attenuation

Various electrical factors, primarily resistance, reduce the power of the signals as they pass through the copper wire. Other factors such as capacitive and inductive reactance drag down the signals at different frequencies. Overall, engineers talk about the attenuation of the signal by the cable. Cable testers measure signal attenuation at several frequency bands.

Typically, a tester measures attenuation on a signal received from a signal injector—a small box about the size of a deck of playing cards that attaches to the far end of the cable. Testers often measure attenuation at 64 KHz, 256 KHz, 512 KHz, 772 KHz, 1 MHz, 2 MHz, 4 MHz, 5 MHz, 8 MHz, 10 MHz, 16 MHz, 20 MHz, 32 MHz, 62.5 MHz, and 100 MHz. Measurements are made up to 16 MHz for Category 3 cables, and up to 100 MHz for Category 4 and 5 cables.

HINT. *When testing twisted-pair cables, be sure the tester switches between all cable pairs in the cable. Sometimes this is a manual task, so it's easy to overlook a pair.*

Attenuation is measured in decibels (dB) and the lower the number, the better. Since the dB scale is logarithmic, even a change of 1 or 2 dB indicates a significant change of power. As an example of the range, the 10Base-T specification allows for a maximum of an 11.5 dB loss in the 5 to 10 MHz band on the 328 feet (100 meters) of wire from the hub to the desktop. The EIA/TIA 568 specification addresses the attenuation problem in more detail. For example, horizontal UTP is measured at ten frequency points, and it allows for a maximum attenuation of 2.8 dB per 1,000 feet at 64 KHz, 7.8 dB per 1,000 feet at 1 MHz, and 40 dB per 1,000 feet at 16 MHz.

Near-end Crosstalk

Near-end crosstalk is the feed-over of electrical energy between wire pairs in the same cable. Cable scanners use a signal injector to properly terminate the far end of the cable, then sweep through a set of frequencies to measure how much signal leaks between the active wire pair carrying the injector's signal and the inactive pair.

Crossed pairs are the most common cause of high levels of near-end crosstalk. The wire map test performed by a cable scanner can identify those pairs for you, but it cannot identify split pairs. Other causes of near-end crosstalk include twisted pairs that are untwisted when attached to cross-connect devices, untwisted patch cables, and cables that are pulled so tightly around a sharp corner that the pairs change position inside the jacket.

Like attenuation, near-end crosstalk is measured in a series of frequency steps going up to 100 MHz. But unlike attenuation, higher numbers are better. A higher near-end crosstalk number indicates a greater difference between the size of the induced signal and the size of the induced crosstalk.

Network Monitoring and Protocol Decoding

Some cable checkers have the ability to monitor network traffic and, in some cases, to even look inside the network frames to report specific types of messages or activity—a function called *protocol decoding.*

Traffic monitoring is particularly useful for detecting unusually high or low levels of traffic. Many cable checkers can generate an audible alarm if the traffic exceeds programmed limits in either direction. You can also often hear a click when a frame goes through the checker—a handy clue to network operation.

Traffic monitoring is also a useful technique for pinpointing loose cables or other problems (such as an Ethernet adapter that malfunctions and broadcasts) without first listening to the cable—a condition called *jabbering.*

You'll need a specific device to monitor an Ethernet network and a different one for a token-ring network. The 10Base-T and token-ring monitors must each act like a node to their respective wiring hubs in order for the hubs to let them access the networks.

Protocol decoding requires a sophisticated program and much more processing power than you'll find in the average cable checker, so these devices cost a lot more. However, if you want to carry all of your troubleshooting devices in one hand, then a cable checker with protocol decoding is a must.

Noise Level Test

While near-end crosstalk is defined as the signals from adjacent wire pairs, many other signals can impose themselves on wire pairs. These signals from commonly found electrical sources often occupy specific frequency bands, as listed in Table 10.1.

Table 10.1

Typical Sources and Frequencies of Near-end Crosstalk

TYPE	RANGE	SOURCE
Low frequency	10 KHz to 150 KHz	Fluorescent lights, heaters
Medium frequency	150 KHz to 100 MHz	Radio, electronic devices, air cleaners
High frequency	16 MHz to 1,000 MHz	Radio and television, computers, electronic devices, motion sensors, radar
Impulse	10 KHz to 100 MHz	Motors, switches, welders, auto ignitions

Electrical noise on a cable is measured in millivolts (one-thousandth of a volt), abbreviated mV. Instead of measuring the peaks of the pulses, the measurement is made on a weighted scale called root mean square (RMS), so typically a cable checker will display a noise reading in mV RMS. The lower the number of millivolts, the less the electrical noise.

When you take a noise reading, you'll have the cables disconnected from the computer equipment. If the cable checker reports high readings, try unplugging electrical devices until you find the source of the noise. Note that simply turning off a device doesn't necessarily work. One of our most frustrating experiences arose from a printer's power supply that generated a large amount of electrical noise and transferred it to a nearby 10Base-T cable when the printer was *off*. When the printer was on, the level of electrical noise was very low. There are always new surprises lurking in every installation.

Programmed Standards

Raw numbers on the attenuation, near-end crosstalk, and noise don't mean much without a reference. If you're buying a cable checker, we strongly suggest getting one that is programmed with reference tables for every standard you will use in your network. This might be IEEE 802.3 10Base-T or IEEE 802.5 token-ring, or it might include high-level tests for EIA/TIA Level 5 cabling. It might even include new evolving standards for 100 megabit and faster signaling over UTP.

Special Features

Cable checkers can come with many special features and management functions. Printing is a feature common in most of them, but look for checkers that print while monitoring; they require more processing power but save time. The ability to print a variety of preprogrammed reports is also a useful option.

Some cable checkers can also serve as cable tracers, sometimes with the addition of a few add-on devices. A cable tracer follows an electrical signal injected into the cable, so you can physically find the cable behind walls. Of course there are less expensive, special-purpose devices that do this, and many people elect to use the special-purpose tracer for this job rather than adding more features to the cable tester.

Remember, standards are constantly evolving, and your cable tester is programmed with information that is likely to change. Some devices offer a method of upgrading the internal software through a modem and a telephone call. This upgradability might cost a little more, but it extends the tester's life and avoids the inconvenience of sending the device back to the factory for an upgrade.

■ Testing Fiber

Optical cable testers cost more than those designed for copper cables, primarily because the test environment is more complex. Fiber-optic cable testers use optical time-domain reflectometry, which depends on the backscattering of light to find the end of the fiber. This backscattering is very weak, and the device must make repeated measurements to ensure accuracy.

It is also much more difficult to measure attenuation in fiber, but it is also less important than in copper cables. A fiber-optic cable tester often includes a power meter to measure the strength of the light signal at the end of the cable. This factor is more important than attenuation, since the power of the light source can often be adjusted within limits to overcome attenuation. This adjustment is part of the power budget computation for the circuit.

■ Baseline and Certification

Cable testers are useful tools for any network manager and are absolutely necessary for every cable installer. A network manager should receive a set of baseline measurements for every cable when the cable system is installed and should periodically check it to ensure the continued quality of the system. Certification to specific IEEE or EIA/TIA standards is critically important to an expanding network and whenever new technology is introduced to the system. Test your cables when you install them and on a periodic basis, and you'll have a secure and effective network system.

- *Motorola Altair*
- *WaveLAN*
- *Xircom Netwave*
- *Printer Connections*
- *Linking Buildings*
- *Wireless Is…*

11

Wireless Communications

"OK 1," the OK Cable dispatcher crackled over the truck's radio, "would you meet the crew at the courthouse? They want to talk to you about a problem."

Willy confirmed the radio call and reviewed what he knew about the courthouse job, which wasn't much. Basically, the county clerk wanted to have a networked PC installed down at the loading dock for checking in packages and getting them distributed without the delay of going through the mail room. OK Cable had installed the original LAN cable system in the clerk's office on the third floor, but the added vertical distance for the new node wouldn't pose a problem.

When Willy pulled up to the courthouse loading dock, he found his crew combing the building plans with the county's network administrator, a retrained deputy sheriff on a disability desk job.

"We got a problem, Willy," his lead installer said. "Between this loading dock and the wiring closet on the new third floor, there's the original first floor built in 1862 with granite walls and marble floors. Of course there are no conduits and practically no space between the walls. I'm glad they don't build buildings like this anymore!"

Willy surveyed the plans, smacked his palm into a granite wall once to confirm that it was really there, shook his head, and then turned to the administrator. "How much data are you going to move over the network? How much network activity will this PC have?"

"Well, they collect all the official mail, packages, and freight for the county here. They probably get three or four shipments in a day, so maybe three to four dozen separate packages or freight shipments. Maybe 50 database entries and about 25 checks against invoices a day, I'd guess." Obviously, the administrator had been doing his homework.

"I'll bet wireless would cost less and do the job," Willy suggested.

The administrator, who was familiar with the pros and cons of police radios, said, "You mean like a cellular telephone or something?"

"Well," Willy replied, "some new cellular telephone systems offer one kind of wireless data system, but that's not what I had in mind. There's a wireless system called WaveLAN—it's from NCR and AT&T so it has lots of backing—that let's you network without cables. It should work great in a situation like this."

The network administrator liked the idea of a wireless link, and Willy promised to work up a proposal. When he returned to his truck to leave, he found the two cable installers leaning against it.

"Wireless?" the bigger one asked with his hands folded across his chest. "Something going on here we should know about?"

Willy nodded sagely. "Yup. You should know that wireless is a good alternative when it's too far or too expensive to install cable. We could install ten normal cable runs for what a single wireless node will cost, but in this case it's a good alternative. Wireless networking isn't as fast as networking over cables and it costs a lot more, so copper cables aren't going to disappear any time soon. But in this case, at least you don't have to spend the next week drilling through granite…assuming the folks in the local committee for historic preservation would let you do that in the first place."

The installers nodded as they took in this new information and then packed up to move to the next job.

Wireless: It's the hottest word in networking. But the term means very different things to different people. There are at least five major types of wireless network connectivity:

- Conference room
- Building/campus
- City/region
- Nationwide (within the United States)
- Worldwide

Each type of wireless networking is supported by a separate group of companies and, to confuse things even more, the categories of networks often overlap. But before we delve too deeply into this topic, we want to make one point clear: *Wireless networks in every category are always an extension of cabled networks, not a replacement.* Few wireless networks are totally wireless.

The rules of physics apply to wireless connections just as they do to cable, but they impose more restrictions on the wireless environment. Radio waves traveling through space face a much more hostile environment than electrons moving through copper. You can have long distance connections, fast connections, and inexpensive connections over wireless, but not all three at once. Distance and signaling speed always work against each other, and raising either of those parameters while holding the other one steady always raises the cost. This relationship means that it's very difficult to field a wireless system that is less expensive than one based on copper cables, and it's also difficult to create one that is faster than copper. In wireless systems, you can generally have it fast, long distance, or inexpensive; pick any two.

So, to use wireless systems successfully, you should deploy them in niche situations where copper is at some disadvantage. The two most fruitful niches for wireless are in contexts where it is awkward to install copper cables and where people need or are willing to pay for mobility.

Any number of situations can arise that make it difficult to install copper cable. For example, you might want to extend the network out to a lone PC in a warehouse or in some other part of the building where the distance limitations exceed the single span of LAN cable. A repeater would solve the problem, but it would also substantially increase the cost of connecting that single node. In this case, a wireless link could be less expensive and much easier to install.

You might also encounter situations where the type of building construction or the inability to gain a construction right-of-way blocks the cable installation. Or, you might need a temporary network connection for a special project. Wireless connections are useful for these cases, too.

Wireless networking and mobile computing serve quite different needs, but so-called "cordless" networking does bring the two technologically closer. Today, the city/region, nationwide, and worldwide connections systems are aimed solely at mobile users. The need for a mobile installation is driven by a different set of factors than the need for wireless connections; because mobile computing network nodes are on the move, direct connection through a fixed cable isn't even a consideration. People who need these services must tolerate low data rates and/or high costs, so cost and performance comparisons with cable are largely moot. Since mobile systems don't compete directly with cable installations, we don't address them in this book, but we do examine several cordless network solutions that compete with and extend cabled services into a local or campus-wide area.

■ Motorola Altair

For several decades, Motorola has been the leading company in very high frequency radio communications in the United States, and it also has a substantial share of that market around the world. Now, the company has applied its radio frequency engineering talents to local area networks. Motorola's Altair system extends Ethernet LAN cabling over radio circuits to link workgroups and to replace or preclude the installation of cabling. The advantages to the Altair system include an installation that takes only seconds and a seamless interface that doesn't require you to modify the network in any way. It works with any LAN operating system.

The Altair system is designed to link segments of cabled LANs, typically between workgroups located on the same floor of a building. A standard configuration is illustrated in Figure 11.1. The system consists of one centrally located control module that acts as the radio communications hub for up to 32 user modules. The simplest system is made up of one control module and one user module, and carries a price tag of several thousand dollars. The control module can attach to a primary LAN cable segment along with up to 32 other cable-attached Ethernet nodes. Each user module connects to a LAN cable along with as many as six other Ethernet nodes.

Figure 11.1

Motorola's Altair system is typically used to link two separate LAN segments with several nodes on each segment. The Altair devices make a direct connection to the network cable at any point and don't directly attach to a computer of any type. Altair works with any computers or networking software.

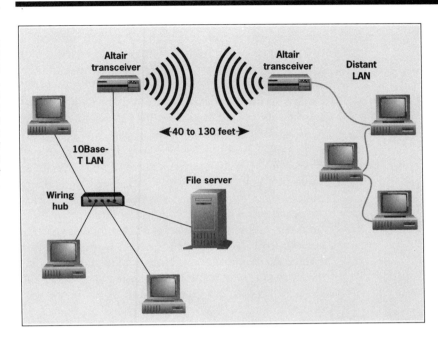

Economically, Altair isn't the best solution for linking a few isolated PCs into the network; NCR's WaveLAN or Xircom's Netwave, described later, are cheaper and better technical solutions for those situations. Price comparisons of the various alternatives are tricky because you must consider the cost of the standard LAN adapters and cabling in each node for Altair, while the WaveLAN and Netwave systems totally replace the LAN adapters and cabling. But Altair excells at linking separate groups of networked PCs when it is too difficult to install a cable between those groups.

Each of the uniquely styled but good-looking Altair modules, which weigh only a few pounds and are about the size of two stacked modems, has its own BNC connector for thin Ethernet cabling and an AUI port for connection to thick Ethernet, 10Base-T unshielded twisted-pair wiring, or fiber-optic cable through an appropriate transceiver. The whole system is essentially plug and play. You just give the Altair units power and an Ethernet connection, and they do the rest.

The units contain their own special purpose microprocessors that perform all of the communications tasks and make the system easy to install and use. They identify and recognize each active device and electronically steer their antenna patterns to produce the best signal strength and avoid signal distortion.

The processor in the control module regulates the transmissions of each user module. This technique insures orderly transmission and reliable communications, but our tests indicate that it imposes a ceiling on throughput.

Because of the transmission regulation and data handling activities taking place in the modules, the Altair system provides a throughput of about a half a megabit per second to a networked PC. The same PC would enjoy two to four times that throughput from a fully cabled system. However, the Altair links suffer only slight degradation under a heavy load and half-a-megabit-per-second throughput will still bring in practically any application program in about the time it takes to shift your gaze from the keyboard to the screen.

Motorola's engineering expertise shows in the use of an extremely high radio frequency and very low power. The units operate at 18 GHz, a frequency band requiring special Federal Communications Commission licenses for operation. The signals in this frequency range are highly directional. The units operate at a power level of 25 milliwatts (25 thousandths of a watt) for very short durations. Both the high frequency and the low power work to reduce the risk of interception and interference. The signals are scrambled but not encrypted according to any U.S. government standard. If security is an issue, Motorola does offer add-on encryption using the Digital Encryption Standard.

The extremely high frequencies don't penetrate thick masonry walls or floors and have a limited ability to pass through plaster and other light construction materials. Under ideal conditions, the control module and user modules can communicate across 130 feet of open space, but that distance might be limited to as little as 40 feet in enclosed offices.

Motorola's Frequency Management Center coordinates with the Federal Communications Commission and controls the assignment of frequencies for the operation of Altair systems. Motorola provides an 800 number and works with Altair owners through faxed messages for quick service.

The Altair system performs at the physical level of the network. The system gathers and transports Ethernet frames; the data inside the frames is inconsequential to the system, so it works with any LAN operating system and transport layer software.

As an aid to interoperability and network management, Motorola offers an option that gives an Altair unit the ability to respond to network management systems using the Simple Network Management Protocol (SNMP). Any SNMP management program, typically running under Windows or on a UNIX workstation, can query the Altair Management Information Base (MIB) to gather information on performance and errors. This significantly improves network troubleshooting capabilities.

The Altair system provides excellent flexibility, and it offers a way to circumvent many barriers to installing LAN cabling. Its ability to work with any

LAN software is a major advantage, but because the costs are higher and the throughput is lower, it should only replace cabled systems in a few installation niches.

■ WaveLAN

NCR's WaveLAN uses an architecture that differs from the Motorola Altair. Altair excels at linking separate groups of nodes; each node in each group uses standard LAN adapters and cables, and the wireless products simply attach to the cable. In contrast, WaveLAN is designed to link each PC into the network using only radio waves. You can establish links between wired workgroups with WaveLAN, but you must add software from Novell or Persoft to make a PC act as a bridge or router. WaveLAN offers good flexibilty and range, and it is only as difficult to install as any standard network adapter.

Each WaveLAN device is a LAN adapter card (available in both ISA and MCA models) that goes into a PC. A minimal system needs two devices. A typical WaveLAN layout is shown in Figure 11.2.

Figure 11.2

WaveLAN installs inside a PC instead of a traditional LAN adapter. In a server-based installation like NetWare, you'll need a WaveLAN adapter in a server to route packets throughout the network.

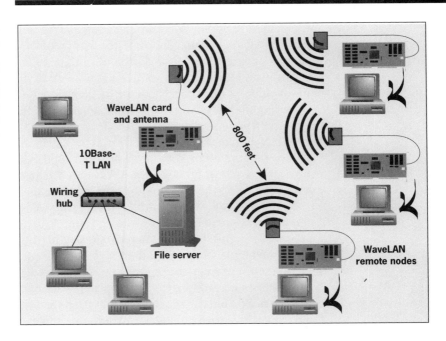

Motorola's Altair can operate regardless of what network operating system or protocols go over the wire, but WaveLAN can't. NCR includes drivers for

NetWare and for the Microsoft/3Com Network Driver Interface Specification (NDIS), so WaveLAN works with Novell's NetWare, many OEM versions of LAN Manager, Banyan Vines, Windows for Workgroups, Artisoft LANtastic version 5.0, and other network operating systems supporting NDIS. NDIS also opens WaveLAN to third party products from companies like ftp Software and Wollongong and to shareware products such as the Clarkson Packet Drivers that you can use to route IP, DECnet, and other packets over WaveLAN.

Each adapter has a small antenna module about the size of a pack of playing cards that attaches to an adapter rather than to a LAN cable. The person using the PC sees a full array of network services just as if the adapter used copper wire instead of airborne radio waves.

The WaveLAN system operates in a frequency band of 902 to 928 MHz, just above the cellular telephone band. Because of the low power (less than half a watt) and the frequency band it uses, these devices do not need a license in the United States and many other countries. The radio waves at this frequency spread out in all directions, but the little antenna module does have some automatic capability to distill interference and seek the best signal.

NCR uses spread spectrum technology in WaveLAN to reduce the potential for receiving and creating interference and to improve the security of the signals. The spread spectrum technology transmits and receives over a bandwidth of several megahertz. The equipment can ignore the common, narrower pulse signals within the bandwidth, even if they are quite strong. NCR offers a Digital Encryption Standard chip to provide tight security for transmissions, but this chip is not for use in products outside the United States.

During the installation you either select or let the NCR software generate a special code that configures the frequency and bandwidth that the WaveLAN systems will use. After installing the first board, you use the same disk to set up the other WaveLAN adapters so they will interoperate. Interestingly, you can establish separate WaveLAN networks that geographically overlap by setting the adapters for different frequencies.

The WaveLAN system literally weaves a network in the air. The adapters listen for an opportunity to transmit and broadcast their messages during a quiet time. For this reason, it's important that all the nodes on the same frequency can hear each other so their signals don't collide. With the normal small antennas, the system can reach out as far as 800 feet. As users of cellular telephones know, signals at these frequencies penetrate most masonry walls and floors, but are blocked by metal, so the effective distance can vary. Larger antennas are available to increase the range of WaveLAN to a mile or more. You can also use two adapters on a separate frequency to establish a link out to a PC that can't hear the rest of the network.

NCR rates WaveLAN at a transmission signaling speed of 2 megabits per second. Our testing shows a consistent throughput of about a half a megabit per second. The system showed little degradation under a heavy load, and it should meet the needs of anyone in an office or warehouse environment.

■ Xircom Netwave

Xircom, an early and consistent leader in LAN adapter technology, has moved into the wireless market, although the company prefers to use the term *cordless* in association with its family of products called Netwave. Netwave excels at providing in-building, high speed, and flexible connections that extend the cabled network.

The Netwave devices include a PCMCIA adapter for suitably equipped laptop computers and devices for all computers that attach to the parallel port. This parallel port connection means that you don't have to open the PC to install Netwave as you do with WaveLAN, and you don't have a separate cost for internal adapters as with Altair. Xircom provides a variety of drivers that make Netwave compatible with all popular network operating systems and with network protocols such as IP and IPX.

The radio in the Netwave system is a 2.4-GHz, frequency-hopping device with a signaling speed of one megabit per second and, because of Xircom's excellent drivers, you can expect throughput of nearly that much—although the real throughput will vary greatly between PCs because of different parallel port designs. Like spread-spectrum, frequency hopping allows the radio to avoid interference and increases capacity, but frequency hopping requires less overall radio spectrum to be as effective. The Netwave transmitters use extremely low power to reduce environmental concerns.

Netwave devices can interoperate from PC to PC at ranges of up to 120 to 150 feet indoors, but Xircom offers an interesting and effective strategy for improving the flexibility and coverage of Netwave-equipped PCs by adding a device called a Netwave Access Point, shown in Figure 11.3. An Access Point joins a network adapter and a radio transceiver together so the radio makes a direct connection to the network. PCs with Netwave can access the network cable through the Access Point to interact with any type of server or service.

For example, you might install an Access Point in each conference room so that laptop-carrying conferees can plug into the network from their seats. Two or three Access Points might cover a warehouse so that people equipped with handheld computers could access the network to check inventory and update the status. One Access Point could economically provide all the network connectivity required by five to ten people in a temporary office.

Figure 11.3

The Xircom Access Point can service a group of Netwave nodes up to 50 meters away. You can have several Access Points in one room if the traffic load is heavy, you can space them throughout a building, or you can position them to cover a specific area like a warehouse or temporary workspace.

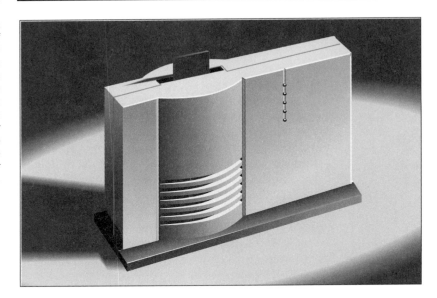

Xircom's Netwave extends the cable system to several categories of network nodes within a building. It offers unmatched portability and complements a high-quality network cable installation.

■ Printer Connections

In some instances, printers can be located where there are no network cables. Two families of products provide wireless printer connections.

The Local Area Wireless Network (LAWN) from O'Neill Communications has been on the market for several years, during which it has proved its reliability. LAWN uses very low-power, spread-spectrum radio broadcasts that can connect PCs to printers over a radius of about 100 feet, and it comes with software that lets you select printers. A small radio transceiver plugs into the serial port of each node. If you need to extend beyond 100 feet, O'Neill offers a repeater that will retransmit another 100 feet.

A somewhat less-expensive and perhaps less-threatening alternative for those who are shy about working around RF energy is available from Argyle Computer Services. Argyle's Lambda Link uses infrared light to link computers to printers. The drawback, of course, is that you must have at least a bounce path for the light between the units. The Lambda Link connects to the PC's parallel port and provides a 9,600-bps link to the printer. The transmitter and receiver each have a 32K buffer, so you get out of your applications quickly after initiating the print job. If multiple print jobs come in from different PCs at the same time, they're stored in the buffers at either end.

You don't need any special software for the Lambda Link, so it works with any Apple, PC, midframe, or other computer. If you have a line-of-sight path of 100 feet or less, the Lambda Link is a nice alternative. It's one of those simple plug-and-play products you always wish for and so rarely seem to get!

■ Linking Buildings

We strongly recommend using fiber-optic cables to link buildings, because it removes the risks of lightning entering the building and of electrocution due to differences in building ground potentials. However, it is sometimes impossible to get the right-of-way to install any type of cable between buildings, and light links can serve to interconnect buildings in another way.

Radio systems can have difficulties penetrating the walls of buildings. Photonics Corporation offers a wireless LAN option that will interface with AppleTalk and relies on light beams instead of the radio waves to carry the mail for WaveLAN, Netwave, and Altair.

The Photonics product, called Building-to-Building Photolink (a special version of the more widely known Photolink) is tuned to operate in the direct sunlight that could interfere with window-to-window operation. Building-to-Building Photolink consists of a pair of transceivers that are simple to install and can carry signals over line of sight distances up to 600 feet.

While the Photonics systems offer relatively slow connectivity at a reasonable price, the top of the optical interbuilding market is dominated by Laser Communications, Inc. (LSI). LSI's Wireless Ethernet L00-18, shown in Figure 11.4, can carry the full 10 megabit-per-second Ethernet signaling on infrared lasers over a distance up to 1 kilometer. A 16 megabit-per-second token-ring version of the product is also available. The cost to establish a building-to-building link can top $20,000, so putting a fiber-optic cable in the ground is still a good alternative. But if you can't get right-of-way and you do have line of sight, then an optical link can be a bargain.

Figure 11.4

The LCI Wireless Ethernet Laser Communications System uses small transceivers to carry data at 10 megabits per second across a line-of-sight path of up to 1 kilometer.

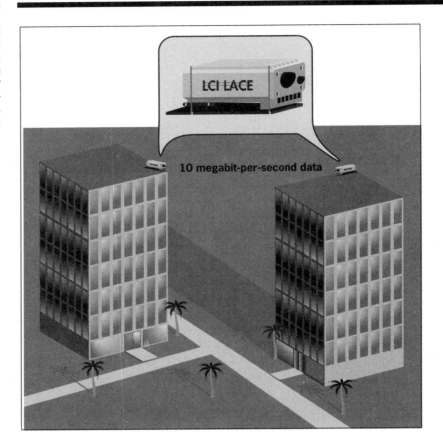

■ Wireless Is...

Anyone who works with network cabling must understand its limitations. Wireless networking in its various forms provides an excellent way around some of those limitations—at a price. We aren't about to retire conduit and crimping tools in favor of wireless systems; instead, wireless connectivity offers new tools for supplementing cabled networks.

■ Appendix

Vendor Directory

■ Network Standards and Cable Systems

AT&T (American Telephone & Telegraph Co.)
295 N. Maple Ave.
Basking Ridge, NJ 07920
800-344-0223

Datapoint Corp.
8400 Datapoint Dr.
San Antonio, TX 78229-8500
800-733-1500; 210-593-7000
Fax: 512-293-7355
Tech support: 512-593-7263

Digital Equipment Corp.
146 Main St.
Maynard, MA 01754-2571
508-493-5111
Fax: 508-493-8780
Tech support: 800-332-8000

Electronic Industries Association
15 Inverness Way E.
Englewood, CO 80112
303-290-9159

Hewlett-Packard Co.
300 Hanover St.
Palo Alto, CA 94304
800-752-0900; 415-857-1501
Tech support: 800-752-0900

IBM Corp.

Contact your local dealer.
800-426-3333

National Fire Protection Association

Batterymarch Park
Quincy, MA 02269-9101
617-770-3000
Fax: 617-984-7056

3Com Corp.

P.O. Box 51845
5400 Bayfront Plaza
Santa Clara, CA 95052-1845
800-638-3266; 408-764-5000
Fax: 408-764-5032
Tech support: 800-876-3266

Underwriters Laboratories

1285 Walt Whitman Rd.
Melville, NY 11747
516-271-6200
Fax: 516-271-8259

■ Wiring Hubs

Acsys Inc.

1372 North McDowell Blvd.
Petaluma, CA 94954
800-462-2797; 707-769-3300

Allied Telesis, Inc.

575 E. Middlefield Rd.
Mountain View, CA 94043
800-424-4284; 415-964-2771
Fax: 415-964-0944
Tech support: 415-964-2771

Asante Technologies

821 Fox Lane
San Jose, CA 95131
800-662-9686; 408-435-8388
Fax: 408-432-1117
Tech support: 800-622-7464

AT&T (American Telephone & Telegraph Co.)

295 N. Maple Ave.
Basking Ridge, NJ 07920
800-432-6600

Cabletron Systems, Inc.

35 Industrial Way
P.O. Box 6257
Rochester, NH 03867
603-332-9400
Fax: 603-332-4616
Tech support: 603-332-9400

David Systems, Inc.

701 E. Evelyn Ave.
Sunnyvale, CA 94086-6527
408-720-8000
Fax: 408-720-9485
Tech support: 408-720-6884

Digital Equipment Corp.

146 Main St.
Maynard, MA 01754-2571
508-493-5111
Fax: 508-493-8780
Tech support: 800-332-8000

D-Link Systems, Inc.

5 Musick
Irvine, CA 92718
800-326-1688; 714-455-1688
Fax: 714-455-2521
Tech support: 714-455-1688

Fibronics International Inc.
33 Riverside Dr.
Pembroke, MA 02359-1978
800-327-9526; 617-826-0099
Fax: 617-826-7745

Hewlett-Packard Co.
300 Hanover St.
Palo Alto, CA 94304
800-752-0900; 415-857-1501
Tech support: 800-752-0900

LANart Corp.
145 Rosemary St.
Needham, MA 02194
800-292-1994; 617-444-1994
Fax: 617-444-3692

Networth, Inc.
8404 Esters Blvd.
Irving, TX 75063
800-544-5255; 214-929-1700
Fax: 214-929-1720
Tech support: 214-929-1700

Optical Data Systems, Inc.
1101 E. Araphro Rd.
Richardson, TX 75081-2336
214-234-6400
Fax: 214-234-4059
Tech support: 214-234-6400

Standard Microsystems Corp.
80 Arky Dr.
Hauppauge, NY 11788
800-SMC-4YOU; 516-435-6000
Tech support: 800-992-4762

SynOptics Communications, Inc.
4401 Great America Pkwy.
P.O. Box 58185
Santa Clara, CA 95052-8185
408-988-2400
Fax: 408-988-5525
Tech support: 408-988-2400

3Com Corp.
P.O. Box 51845
5400 Bayfront Plaza
Santa Clara, CA 95052-1845
800-638-3266; 408-764-5000
Fax: 408-764-5032
Tech support: 800-876-3266

■ Cable Manufacturers and Suppliers

Amp Inc.
P.O. Box 3608
Harrisburg, PA 17105-3608
800-522-6752; 717-564-0100
Fax: 717-986-7575
Tech support: 800-522-6752

Anixter Bros., Inc.
4711 Golf Rd.
Skokie, IL 60076
708-677-2600

AT&T (American Telephone & Telegraph Co.)
295 N. Maple Ave.
Basking Ridge, NJ 07920
800-344-0223

Belden Electronic Wire and Cable
P.O. Box 1980
Richmond, IN 47375
319-983-5200

Champlain Cable

12 Hercules Dr.
Colchester, VT 05446
800-451-5162
Fax: 802-655-2025

Comm/Scope, Inc.

P.O. Box 879
3642 Hwy. 70 East
Claremont, NC 28610
800-982-1708; 704-459-5000
Fax: 704-459-5099

Dupont Cable

8659 Baypine Rd., Ste. 305
Jacksonville, FL 32256
904-733-2548

International Connectors and Cable Corporation

16624 Edwards Rd.
Cerritos, CA 90701
800-333-7776; 310-926-0734
Fax: 310-926-5290

Mod-Tap

285 Ayers Rd.
P.O. Box 706
Harvard, MA 01451
508-772-5630
Fax: 508-772-2011
Tech support: 508-772-4884

Mohawk Wire & Cable Corp.

9 Mohawk Dr.
Leominster, MA 01453
800-422-9961; 508-537-9961
Fax: 508-537-4358

■ Cable Connectors

Amp Inc.
P.O. Box 3608
Harrisburg, PA 17105-3608
800-522-6752; 717-564-0100
Fax: 717-986-7575
Tech support: 800-522-6752

Black Box Corporation
P.O. Box 12800
Pittsburgh, PA 15241
412-746-5500
Tech support: 412-746-5500

Graybar
Contact your nearest dealer.

Krone, Inc.
6950 S. Tucson Way
Englewood, CO 80112
800-992-9901; 303-790-2619
Fax: 303-790-2117

Mod-Tap
285 Ayers Rd.
P.O. Box 706
Harvard, MA 01451
508-772-5630
Fax: 508-772-2011
Tech support: 508-772-4884

Momaco, Inc.
1875 W. Fullerton Ave.
Chicago, IL 60614
312-384-5575
Fax: 312-384-6080

North Hills Electronics, Inc.
Alexander Pl.
Glen Cove, NY 11542
516-671-5700
Fax: 516-759-3327

Ortronics

595 Greenhaven Rd.
Pawcatuck, CT 06379
203-599-1760
Fax: 203-599-1774

Panduit

17301 Ridgeland Ave.
Tinley Park, IL 60477-0981
708-532-1800
Fax: 708-532-1811

Unicom Electric, Inc.

11980 Telegraph Rd., Ste. 103
Santa Fe Springs, CA 90670
310-946-9650
Fax: 310-946-7473

■ Cable Test Equipment

Beckman Industrial Corp.

3883 Ruffin Rd.
San Diego, CA 92123-1898
800-854-2708
Fax: 619-268-0172

Datacom Technologies, Inc.

11001 31st Place W.
Everett, WA 98204
800-468-5557; 206-355-0590
Fax: 206-290-1600
Tech support: 800-468-5557

John Fluke Manufacturing Co., Inc.

P.O. Box 9090
Everett, WA 98206-9090
800-443-5853; 206-347-6100
Fax: 206-356-5116
Tech support: 800-443-5853

Microtest, Inc.

4747 North 22nd St.
Phoenix, AZ 85016-4708
800-526-9675; 602-957-6400
Fax: 602-957-6414
Tech support: 602-957-6400

Mod-Tap

285 Ayers Rd.
P.O. Box 706
Harvard, MA 01451
508-772-5630
Fax: 508-772-2011
Tech support: 508-772-4884

Wavetek Instruments Division

9045 Balboa Ave.
San Diego, CA 92123
800-854-2708; 619-279-2200

■ Cable Tools

General Machine Products

3111 Old Lincoln Hwy.
Trevose, PA 19053-4996
215-357-5500
Fax: 215-357-6216

Jensen Tools, Inc.

7815 S. 46th St.
Phoenix, AZ 85044-5399
800-426-1194
Fax: 800-366-9662

Mod-Tap

285 Ayers Rd.
P.O. Box 706
Harvard, MA 01451
508-772-5630
Fax: 508-772-2011
Tech support: 508-772-4884

■ National Cable and Connector Retailers

Anco Corporation
140 North Palm St.
Brea, CA 92621
800-545-ANCO; 714-992-9000
Fax: 714-992-1672

Black Box Corporation
P.O. Box 12800
Pittsburgh, PA 15241
412-746-5500
Tech support: 412-746-5500

Data Comm Warehouse
1720 Oak St.
P.O. Box 301
Lakewood, NJ 08701-9885
800-328-2261
Fax: 908-363-4823

Glasgal Communications, Inc.
151 Veterans Dr.
Northvale, NJ 07647
201-768-8082
Fax: 201-768-2947

Graybar
Contact your dealer.

Inmac
2465 Augustine Dr.
P.O. Box 58031
Santa Clara, CA 95052-8031
800-547-5444

Newark Electronics
4801 N. Ravenswood Ave.
Chicago, IL 60640-4496
312-784-5100

One Network Place
 4711 Golf Rd.
 Skokie, IL 60076
 800-622-6415
 Fax: 800-622-6418

South Hills Datacom
 Cord Cable Company
 760 Beechnut Dr.
 Pittsburgh, PA 15205
 800-245-6215
 Fax: 412-921-2254
 Tech support: 800-248-TECH

Specialized Products Company
 3131 Premier Dr.
 Irving, TX 75063
 800-866-5353; 214-550-1923
 Fax: 800-234-8286; 214-550-8286

■ Wireless Networking Products

Argyle Computer Services
 14805 Silverstone Dr.
 Silver Springs, MD 20905
 301-236-9513

Laser Communications, Inc.
 1848 Charter Lane, Ste. F
 P.O. Box 10066
 Lancaster, PA 17605-0066
 717-394-8634
 Fax: 717-396-9831

Motorola, Inc. (Wireless Enterprises Division)
 1201 E. Wiley Rd., Ste. 103
 Schaumburg, IL 60173
 800-233-0877; 708-576-1600
 Fax: 708-576-0710

NCR Corp.

1700 S. Patterson Blvd.
Dayton, OH 45479-0001
800-272-6270; 513-445-5000
Fax: 513-445-4184
Tech support: 800-272-6270

O'Neill Communications, Inc.

607 Horsham Rd.
Horsham, PA 19044
800-624-5296; 215-957-5408
Fax: 215-957-6633
Tech support: 215-957-5408

Photonics Corporation

2940 N. First St.
San Jose, CA 95134
800-628-3033; 408-955-7930
Fax: 408-955-7950

Xircom, Inc.

26025 Mureau Rd.
Calabasas, CA 91302
800-438-9472; 818-878-7600
Direct sales: 800-874-7875
Fax: 818-878-7630
Tech support: 800-874-4428

■ Glossary

active hub   In ARCnet, a wiring hub used to amplify network transmissions for greater distances. (*See also* passive hub.)

Advanced Communications Service (ACS)   A large data communications network developed by AT&T.

alternating current (AC)   An electrical signal or current which reverses direction periodically. AC is the form of electrical power found in residential and commercial buildings.

American National Standards Institute (ANSI)   An organization that develops and publishes standards for codes, data alphabets, and signaling schemes.

Anixter   A worldwide manufacturer of wiring system products. Anixter developed a model for cable classification.

ARCnet (Attached Resources Computing Networks)   A networking architecture (marketed by Datapoint Corp. and other vendors) using a token passing bus architecture, usually on coaxial cable.

ARCNETPLUS   A 20-megabit signaling scheme version of ARCnet developed and marketed by Datapoint Corp.

asynchronous   A method of transmission in which the time intervals between characters are not required to be equal. Start and stop bits may be added to coordinate the transfer of characters.

Asynchronous Transfer Mode (ATM)   A method of network transmission using very small packets. ATM's primary advantage is the ability to carry time-sensitive packets, such as video or voice, without substantial delay. ATM networks will expand smoothly from local to wide area networks.

attachment unit interface (AUI)   A 15-pin D-connector located on the network adapter used to connect cables to fiber-optic, coaxial, or 10Base-T transceivers.

attenuation   The decrease in power of a signal as it travels along the cable.

attenuator   A device that is used to intentionally decrease, or attenuate, the signal. In fiber optics, a device that dims the light passing through it.

balun (BALanced UNbalanced)   An impedance-matching device that connects a balanced line (such as twisted-pair) and an unbalanced line (such as coaxial cable).

bandwidth   The range of frequencies a circuit will pass. Analog circuits typically have a bandwidth limited to that of a human voice (about 3KHz). The square waves of digital sound require higher bandwidth. The higher the transmission rate, the greater the bandwidth requirement. Fiber-optic and coaxial cables have excellent bandwidth.

baseband   A network that transmits signals as a direct-current pulse rather than as variations in a radio frequency signal.

Bell Standard Practices (BSP)   A set of procedures designed before the breakup of the Bell Systems. The BSP described in detail how installers should cut, twist, and attach every wire, and how to secure every cable span.

BNC connector   A small coaxial connector with a half-twist locking shell. BNC is an acronym for Bayone-Neill-Concelman.

broadband signaling   A network that carries information riding on carrier waves rather than directly as pulses, and provides greater capacity at the cost of higher complexity.

broadcast   To send a message to all stations or an entire class of stations connected to the network.

Carrier Sense Multiple Access with Collision Detection (CSMA/CD)   A media-sharing scheme in which stations listen in to what's happening on the network media; if the cable is not in use, the station is permitted to transmit its message. CSMA is often combined with a means of performing collision detection, hence CSMA/CD.

cladding   The material, usually glass, that surrounds the core of the optical fiber. Light bounces off the interface between the cladding and fiber and returns to the fiber.

coaxial cable   A type of network media. Coaxial cable contains a copper inner conductor surrounded by plastic insulation and then a woven copper or foil shield.

Common Management Information Protocol (CMIP)   A structure for formatting messages and transmitting information between reporting devices and data collection programs. Developed by the International Standards Organization and designated as ISO 9596.

conductor   Any material that is capable of carrying an electrical current.

controlled access unit (CAU)   The IBM name for an intelligent wiring hub used in IBM Token-Ring networks.

Copper Distributed Data Interface (CDDI)   A specification developed by Crescendo Communications that uses the FDDI techniques over unshielded twisted-pair.

cross-connect device   A device that terminates a cable or group of cables and makes the termination available for interconnection to other cables.

crosstalk   The spillover of a signal from one channel to another. In data communications it is very disruptive. In cable systems, crosstalk comes from adjacent cable pairs.

data-link layer   The second layer of the OSI model. Protocols functioning in this layer manage the flow of data leaving a network device and work with the receiving station to ensure that the data arrives safely.

direct current (DC)   An electrical current which travels in only one direction. DC is most commonly used in electronic circuits.

distortion   Any change to the transmitted signal. May be caused by crosstalk, delay, attenuation, or other factors.

distributed capacitance   The electrical property of capacitance developed within a cable that stores a direct current charge while passing an alternating current charge. This has the effect of diminishing the low frequency portion of transmitted signals.

distributed inductance   The electrical property of inductance developed within a cable that stores an alternating current charge while passing a direct current charge. This has the effect of diminishing the high frequency portion of transmitted signals.

DIX connector   The connector used on the AUI socket and the transceiver cable.

EIA RS-232   An electrical standard for the interconnection of equipment, established by the Electrical Industries Association. (*See also* serial port.)

EIA/TIA-568   The EIA/TIA's Standard for Commercial Building Telecommunications Wiring. The EIA/TIA-568 standard describes a set of performance classifications and installation parameters for network cable. This standard is scheduled to be replaced with the similar EIA/TIA-568A.

EIA/TIA-569   The Commercial Building Standard for Telecommunication Pathways and Spaces.

EIA/TIA-570   The Residential and Light Commercial Telecommunications Wiring Standard.

EIA/TIA-606   The Administration Standard for the Telecommunications Infrastructure of Commercial Buildings. The EIA/TIA-606 describes the method for numbering and labeling cabling, pathways, and spaces.

electromagnetic interference/radio frequency interference (EMI/RFI)   Outside sources of potential intereference on your network cable. EMI/RFI sources include radio transmitters, electric relays and switches, thermostats, and fluorescent lights.

Electronic Industries Association (EIA)   An organization of U.S. manufacturers of electronics parts and equipment. The organization develops industry standards for the interface between data processing and communications equipment.

Ethernet   A network cable and access protocol scheme originally developed by Xerox that uses a carrier-sense multiple access (CSMA) media access control scheme. Described and expanded in the IEEE 802.3 standards.

fault   A physical or logical break in a communications link.

Fiber Distributed Data Interface (FDDI)   A specification for fiber-optic networks operating at 100 megabits per second. FDDI uses wiring hubs, and the hubs are prime candidates for monitoring and control devices.

fiber optics   A data-transmission method that uses light pulses sent over glass cables.

fiber-optic interrepeater link (FOIRL)   IEEE specification for running Ethernet over fiber-optic cable. Typically used between transceivers or between wiring hubs. Easily confused but not interoperable with devices conforming to 10Base-F specifications.

four-wire circuit   A transmission arrangement where two half-duplex circuits (two wires each) are combined to make one full-duplex circuit.

full-duplex   The ability for communications to flow both ways over a communications link at the same time.

ground   An electrically neutral contact point.

half-duplex Alternating transmissions: Each station can either transmit or receive, but not do both simultaneously.

Hertz (Hz) The number of electrical cycles (vibrations) per second. An Hz is equal to one cycle per second.

horizontal wiring The cable that runs between each wall jack and its associated wiring closet.

IBM type 1 connector A connector used with shielded twisted-pair cable in a token-ring network.

IEEE 802.3 An IEEE standard describing CSMA/CD networking. The standard contains many subelements, including 10Base-T.

IEEE 802.5 An IEEE specification that describes a LAN using 4- or 16-megabit-per-second signaling, token passing media access control, and a physical ring topology. It is used by IBM's Token-Ring systems. (*See also* Token-Ring.)

impedance A complex opposition to the flow of an alternating current in a circuit. Elements of distributed inductance, distributed capacitance, and resistance combine to create impedance.

Institute of Electrical and Electronics Engineers (IEEE) A standards-making organization responsible for many LAN-based standards and rules.

integrated services digital network (ISDN) As officially defined by CCITT, "a limited set of standard interfaces to a digital communications network." The result is a network that supplies end users with voice, data, and certain image services on end-to-end digital circuits. The plan is to provide two 64-kilobit-per-second channels and one 16-kbps channel over digital telephone lines to desktops worldwide.

interface The interconnection point—usually between equipment.

International Consultive Committee on Telephone and Telegraph (CCITT) An international organization responsible for developing communications standards.

International Standards Organization, Paris (ISO) An organization that developed the seven-layer Open Standards Interconnect model.

jacket The outside layer of network cabling. The jacket protects the cable, and usually carries markings describing the cable. Various cable jackets are available for interior use, buried use, and use in areas where smoke or flames would create dangerous fumes.

Kevlar   An aramid fiber that is used to provide crush resistance and pulling strength in a fiber-optic cable. Kevlar is a trademark of the DuPont Company.

linear bus topology   A topology where the nodes connect to the cable and the cable proceeds in a linear fashion between the nodes.

local area network (LAN)   A computer communications system limited to no more than a few miles and using high-speed (2-100 megabit per second) connections.

main distribution frame (MDF)   MDF, also called the cross-connection point, is a wiring point used primarily to distribute circuits coming in from outside the building.

Management Information Base (MIB)   A database containing specific elements of information pertaining to the operation and performance of a specific piece of equipment, program, or function. A processor holds data in the format of the MIB until it is polled for the information. An MIB is a key part of the SNMP management system.

media   The cabling or wiring used to carry network signals. Typical examples are coax, fiber-optic, and twisted-pair wire. Plural of medium.

media access control (MAC)   The rules that LAN workstations abide by to avoid data collisions when sending signals over shared network media. Often used as "the MAC layer" to mean the access control layer of protocols.

media attachment unit (MAU)   A transceiver that attaches to the AUI port on an Ethernet adapter and provides electrical and mechanical attachment to fiber, twisted-pair, or other media.

MIC connector   The Medium Interface Connector (MIC) was adopted by ANSI as part of the FDDI architecture. The MIC connector contains two fibers and is keyed to prevent attaching the MIC the wrong way.

micron   One micrometer, or one millionth of a meter.

multimode fiber   A fiber large enough to carry multiple modes of light. The type of fiber most commonly used in local area networks.

National Electrical Code (NEC)   A code established by the National Fire Protection Association. The NEC basically describes the classification and installation of electrical power and signal cables.

N-connector   The large-diameter connector used with thick Ethernet cable.

near-end crosstalk (NEXT)   Interference measured on a wire that is located adjacent to the wire in which the signal is being sent.

NetView   A network-management product designed by IBM and 3Com. NetView is a specific network-management and control architecture that relies heavily on mainframe data collection programs but also incorporates PC-level products running under OS/2.

network   A continuing connection between two or more computers that facilitates the sharing of files and resources.

nominal velocity of propogation (NVP)   The ratio between the speed of an electrical pulse in a specific type of cable and the speed of light.

ohm   Primarily, a unit of resistance, but also can be used to express impedance.

on-line   Connected to a network or host computer system.

Open Systems Interconnection (OSI) reference model   A model for networks, developed by the International Standards Organization, that divides the network functions into seven layers. Each layer builds on the services provided by those under it.

OpenView   Hewlett-Packard's suite of network management applications, a server platform, and support services. OpenView is based on HP-UX, which complies with AT&T's UNIX system.

passive hub   A wiring hub that does not amplify network transmissions, but only segments the transmissions between several nodes (*See also* active hub.)

patch panel   A panel built into a cabinet that contains jacks which terminate individual cables. Jumper cables make connections between the individual jacks. A patch panel makes it easy to change network cable connections.

polyvinyl chloride (PVC)   Used as an insulating material in coaxial cables between the solid core and the outside braid.

premise distribution system (PDS)   A building-wide telecommunications cabling system. AT&T, Northern Telecom, and other vendors have specified PDS architectures.

private branch exchange (PBX)   A telephone system serving a specific location. Many PBX systems can carry network data without the use of modems.

protocol   A specification that describes the rules and procedures that products should follow to perform activities on a network, such as transmitting data. Protocols allow products from different vendors to communicate on the same network.

punch-down block   A central termination point for twisted-pair cable.

repeater   In Ethernet, a device that amplifies and regenerates signals so they can travel farther on a cable.

RG-58   A coaxial cable connector that has a 50-ohm impendance and is used with thin Ethernet.

RJ-45   An 8-pin connector used for data transmissions over telephone twisted-pair wire.

RG-62   A coaxial cable connector that has a 93-ohm impedance and is used with ARCnet.

sag   A decrease of below 80 percent in normal line voltage. Also known as a brownout.

SC connector   An acronym for style connector, this connector is often used in cable splices.

screened twisted-pair (SCTP)   Twisted-pair cabling with an outer foil shield to reduce EMI. It has performance and operating characteristics similar to UTP.

serial port   An I/O port that transmits data 1 bit at time, as compared to a parallel port, which transmits multiple (usually 8) bits simultaneously. EIA RS-232 supports serial signaling.

Shielded Distributed Data Interface (SDDI)   A specification promoted by IBM and other vendors to run FDDI protocols over shielded twisted-pair cable.

shielded twisted-pair (STP)   Twisted-pair cabling with an overall shield to prevent the entry of outside interference, and individually shielded and twisted-pairs to prevent crosstalk.

Simple Network Management Protocol (SNMP)   A structure for formatting messages and transmitting information between reporting devices and data-collection programs. Developed jointly by the Department of Defense, industry, and the academic community as part of the TCP/IP protocol suite.

single-mode fiber   A fiber that has a very small core, allowing only one mode of light to enter and propagate. Single-mode fibers do not suffer modal dispersion and are the best choice for very long runs requiring high data speeds.

SMA connector   A type of fiber-optic connector used extensively in telephone installations before the introduction of the ST-type connector. It is still popular. Originally an acronym for Sub-Minature Assembly.

spike   A power impulse that lasts between 0.5 and 100 microseconds and possesses an amplitude over 100 percent of peak line voltage.

spread-spectrum   A method of radio transmission that spreads the signal out over a wide bandwidth, typically 1 or more megahertz. Spread-spectrum signals are much less susceptable to interference from pulse noise and from other radio signals. Widely used in short-range wireless LAN systems.

ST connector   A fiber-optic connector developed and trademarked by AT&T, it is the type of connector most commonly used in fiber local area networks. The acronym orginally stood for Straight Tip.

star topology   A network connection method that brings all links to a central node, or wiring hub.

station cable   The cable that connects the network node to the wall jack.

surge   A voltage increase above 110 percent of normal power voltage.

Systimax   AT&T's specification for installing and planning network cable.

tap   A connector that couples to a cable without blocking the passage of signals down the cable.

10Base-F   IEEE's specification for running CSMA/CD networking (Ethernet) over fiber-optic cable. This specification contains several subcategories for low-cost, plastic, interrepeater, and other links.

10Base-T   IEEE's specifications for running CSMA/CD networking (Ethernet) over unshielded twisted-pair cable. (*See also* IEEE 802.3.)

10Base-2   IEEE's specifications for running CSMA/CD networking (Ethernet) over thin coaxial cable.

10Base-5   IEEE's specifications for running CSMA/CD networking (Ethernet) over thick coaxial cable.

T-connector   A coaxial connector, shaped like a T, that connects two thin Ethernet cables while supplying an additional connector for a network interface card.

thick Ethernet   A cabling system using large-diameter, relatively stiff cable to connect transceivers. The transceivers connect to the nodes through flexible multi-wire cable.

thin Ethernet   A cabling system using a thin and flexible coaxial cable to connect each node to the next node in line.

time-domain reflectometry (TDR)   The technique of sending an electric pulse down a cable and then timing its reflection back from the other end. Most cable scanners use TDR to determine the length of the cable.

token   A message that gives a node permission to transmit.

token passing   An access protocol in which a special message (token) circulates among the network nodes giving them permission to transmit.

token-ring   Refers to the wire and the access protocol scheme whereby stations relay packets in a logical ring configuration. This architecture, pioneered by IBM, is described in the IEEE 802.5 standards.

topology   The map of the network. The physical topology describes how the wires or cables are laid out, and the logical or electrical topology describes how the messages flow.

transceiver   In networks, a device that connects a specific type of cable, such as coax or fiber, to a network adapter card through the AUI connector.

Transmission Control Protocol/Internet Protocol (TCP/IP)   Originally developed by the Department of Defense, this set of communications protocols has evolved since the late 1970s. Because network communications programs supporting these protocols are available on so many different computer systems, they have become an excellent way to connect different types of computers over networks.

trunk segment   In Ethernet, a piece of cable with a terminator at each end.

twisted-pair wiring   Cable comprised of two wires twisted together to provide increased bandwidth. Some telephone wiring—but by no means all—is twisted-pair.

Underwriters Laboratories (UL)   An organization, founded by the National Board of Fire Underwriters, that specifies safety standards.

uninterruptible power supply (UPS)   A backup device designed to provide an uninterrupted power source in the event of a power failure. UPSs should be installed on all file servers and wiring hubs.

unshielded twisted-pair (UTP)   Twisted-pair cabling that does not have individual or overall shielding.

vertical wiring   The cable that forms the backbone between the wiring closets and the main cross-connection point in the building.

volt   A unit measure of electrical force.

wiring hub   A cabinet, usually mounted in a wiring closet, that holds connection modules for various kinds of cabling. The hub contains electronic circuits that retime and repeat the signals on the cable. The hub may also contain a microprocessor that monitors and reports on network activity.

■ Index